A Better Story

Sermons from the Book of Genesis

Zach Weihrauch

First published by Dog Ear Publishing
4011 Vincennes Rd
Indianapolis, IN 46268
www.dogearpublishing.net

ISBN: 978-1-4575-4517-7

This book is printed on acid-free paper.

Printed in the United States of America

To the original fourteen members of Gateway Heights Church. You said no to so many things in order to say yes to a gospel witness in your city. I will be forever grateful.

Acknowledgments

This book is a collection of sermons that I preached at Gateway Heights Church in 2013 and 2014. The present form of those sermons, and any and all eloquence within, owes its existence to the tireless and intelligent efforts of many people. Evan and Heather Storey did the unenviable work of turning my rhetorical efforts into something readable. Patrick Muscenti did the majority of the editing work. All of this was done under the watchful care of Dr. Cory Wilson, whom I have learned to run any and all things by for the good of myself and the church.

Introduction

All people who have ever lived, regardless of time, place, or culture, haved looked for a larger story by which they can make sense of their lives. The search for this metanarrative takes many shapes and forms, with some turning to religion, others to politics, romance, achievement, and many other places. We all may turn to different places in our efforts to find a larger story, but the search is a consistent and constant part of humanity.

In my generation, it has become popular to eschew the all-encompassing human narratives in favor of the more personal and subjective narrative. The culture encourages each of us to find his or her own story to give individual lives the meaning that we are all looking for in life. We are told from the time we are in grade school that we are snowflakes who are unique and special and that life is the ongoing discovery of just how unique and special we really are and the ongoing process of each one of us deciding what the words "unique" and "special" even mean to us.

Despite the freedom that this newfound approach seems to offer, I am finding that many of us find this path to be a kind of candy-coated poison. We run headlong into freedom only to find that the narratives we have constructed for ourselves don't provide the meaning that we are looking for. I minister to a young congregation full of the country's best and brightest undergraduates, graduate students, and young professionals who find themselves increasingly disenfranchised with their snowflake status. They sit in corner offices, the pursuit of which has eaten up the first thirty years of their lives, and find that they are dissatisfied with what their narrative of ambition has provided them. Marriages buckle under the weight of being asked to provide life's meaning, and infertility threatens to ruin the individual's narrative of choice before it even gets started.

Increasingly, I find that my neighbors are growing restless with their own stories and find themselves with only anxiety and depression where they were told they would find meaning and joy. They show up to my church, to my office, and sometimes even to my home with the same question on their minds—"Is there a larger story in which I can find the meaning and joy I feel that I am meant to know?"

They are often surprised when I tell them that the answer to that question is found where they were least likely to look, in the Bible, where the larger metanarrative—a truly better story—of the person and work of Jesus Christ is found. In the Scriptures, these individuals find that their lives take on meaning not when they claim their snowflake status or seek to be the main characters in their own stories but when they relinquish their claims to stardom and seek rather to identify themselves within the story of what God is doing in the world through Jesus Christ.

This is the argument of the book of Genesis: God is writing a larger narrative that will lead to the ongoing glory of his Son Jesus Christ, and in his grace, he has chosen to unite that glory to the good of his people so the story has room for us in it. Genesis is the beginning of this metanarrative, and as such, its goal is to challenge the opposing stories we are prone to believe and to call us to join with Seth in "calling on the name of the Lord" (Genesis 4:26)—not just on the name of the God of Abraham, Isaac, and Jacob but also on the name of the one whom God promised would come to put the world back together (Genesis 3:16)—Jesus. Every event in Genesis derives its meaning from this goal, and thus every event derives its meaning from him. Genesis is a challenge to us to find true meaning and purpose by losing our individual stories in the greater whole of the story of Jesus.

In this way, the challenge of Genesis to us today is not unlike its challenge to its original audience. As Moses led God's people into a "promised land," they would find themselves surrounded by many competing narratives that would serve as arguments to lead them to find their identity in something other than God. Genesis served as the opening salvo of God to remind them that he and he alone was writing the story of the universe. Genesis begins a better story that will lead you to find the meaning and purpose that you are looking for in your life. This book is an effort to show that truth, using each story to provide a greater glimpse into the story of God and its implications on our lives.

Originally, this book was a series of thirty-two sermons that I preached at Gateway Heights Church. For the purpose of time and space, it has been reduced to the twenty sermons most necessary to display a cohesive vision of Genesis as an argument to join the story of God through faith in Jesus Christ. May God be glorified and the larger story of Jesus be increased!

Zach Weihrauch

Chapter 1

Music or Material

Understanding the Foundation of Our World

Genesis 1:1–3

There are different kinds of questions, and different places you go to get answers to those questions. When you have a particular question, it is important that you go to the right place to get the correct answer. Say you are at the hospital and your doctor gives you a terminal diagnosis. Your doctor says you have this rare form of cancer and you have three months to live. There are lots of questions you are going to ask. There are logistical questions, which some people at the hospital are equipped to answer. Social workers and counselors are going to walk you through how to make the right decisions, how to work through the process of being sick, of passing away, and of making sure that process goes well for those you care about. If you have questions about what is going on in your body or what is going on biologically, the doctor is equipped to answer those questions. Then there are more existential questions, like "What happens when you die?" "Why me?" and "Why is there death?" Those are a different kind of question. You can think about your diagnosis and ask logistical questions: "What am I going to do? What is the next step?" Next, there are physical questions: "What is going on in my body?" Finally, there are metaphysical or spiritual questions: "What happens when I die? Why am I here in the first place? Why would this happen to me?" There are particular kinds of questions, and you have go to particular places to find those answers, and if you go to the wrong place to get a question answered, you are in real trouble.

Genesis is a book of the Bible over which there is a lot of confusion and debate. The book of Genesis itself, part one of a five-part series, is massive, and yet so much of the conversation about Genesis centers around chapters one and two. Much of the confusion stems from the problem of asking the wrong questions of the wrong people. The creation account in the opening chapters of Genesis was not written to primarily answer biological, mathematical, physical, or chemical questions. We know this because Moses, who wrote Genesis, predated modern science by several thousand years. Today, many of us are coming to Genesis, asking questions of Moses that he is not trying to answer, and then we are getting frustrated at the meager answers we are scraping out. Moses wrote Genesis not to answer logistical or even physical questions but to answer metaphysical questions and spiritual questions.

The book of Genesis begins the Biblical story. If you read the Bible from beginning to end, you will see a narrative progression running through the entirety of Scripture. Genesis and the Bible's metanarrative is aiming at spiritual questions. I do not mean that in the narrative of the Bible that physical things are never explained. Sometimes, physical things are explained. It is similar to when a writer writes a particular scene in a novel. Whatever he tells you is true. If he says, "The sun is setting," then the sun is setting, but the point of the book is not in one sentence to detail the sun setting. Sometimes in the narrative of scripture, we get to physical realities; whatever the Bible says about those physical realities is true. Wherever the Bible delves into the physical, it always gets it correct. In explaining this, I don't mean that Moses is inferior to scientists, just that he has a different agenda.

When we read the book of Genesis, we have to focus on what the author is trying to say and what the original audience wanted to know, so that when we connect those things we find out what is really there. Moses is writing the book of Genesis for this reason: the people of Israel are getting ready to cross into the promised land. When they get there, they will encounter a variety of people who have a variety of world views, a variety of philosophies, and variety of ideas about God. Moses is writing down the truth for God's people so that when they enter the land they will know the answer to questions like: "Who is God?" "Why are we here?" "What is the purpose of life?" When they get into the promised land, they will be surrounded by people who answer those questions differently. Moses is taking the time to write the first five books of the Bible to say, "When your child asks you why this…" you can take them back to Genesis and Exodus and you will answer them from the text.

The book of Genesis is a polemic; it is an argument for monotheism. But it is not just any kind of monotheism; it shows us the one true God. That is why it was written. And even though Genesis is not primarily about physical questions, that does not make it inferior to science. It actually makes Genesis superior to science. Sometimes, the supposed conflict between science and Genesis is simply because we are trying to bring Genesis down and bring science up. We are trying to get Genesis to deal with the physical, while it is telling us, "I want to deal with the metaphysical." Meanwhile, we are trying to say to science, "You can tell me what is going on in my body, but can you tell me why I have a body? You can tell me there is a universe, but can you tell me if there is meaning in the universe?"

The Bible is an argument that reveals what it means to be human, why there is a universe, what the meaning of life is, and who creates and sustains us all. This argument stood over and against the polytheism of Moses's day, but in our day, it takes its stand against naturalism, secularism, and pluralism. I would define naturalism as the idea that science answers not only the physical questions but also the metaphysical questions. Science can tell us why the universe operates in a particular way and why there actually is a universe. This world-view is an argument for truth, just like any other worldview.

In Genesis, all we need are the first three verses to find a few of our deeper questions answered—questions that human beings have been asking from the beginning of time. If you go back two thousand years, you will not find people asking primarily biological, physical, or chemical questions, but you will find them asking spiritual questions. Wherever there have been people, there have been these questions. Genesis starts off by saying, in essence, "Here is why you are asking these questions, and here is how you can be pointed toward an answer." This is why we must be driven to the book of Genesis, and this is why we must be driven to the biblical story.

To display the answers the Bible gives to these spiritual questions, I want to contrast the biblical idea of music with materialism. By materialism, I simply mean the idea that we come from nothing and we are going to nothing. Materialism holds that the world is a closed system and there is only biology, only physics, only chemistry, and only matter. It is the naturalistic and scientific view of the world. I want to show how the Bible says this worldview is not true, but, more specifically, I also want to show you how the Bible portrays a better world-view by picking up on rhythms that are happening in our own hearts. In Genesis, the Bible is telling us that the music we all dance to in our hearts and in our own souls is evidence that its worldview is true. The Bible displays three rhythms to which our hearts dance. They are the relational rhythm, the artistic rhythm, and the mechanical rhythm.

The Relational Rhythm

It is common for each one of us to say love is ultimate in the world. Songs say it, books say it, paintings say it, and our own experience says it. It is better to be poor and have friends than to be rich and lonely. Why is it that deep down, we say love is ultimate? Why is it that we say relationships are ultimate? Why is it that we say things like "Love can fix our world" and "If we could all just love each other, the world would be a better place"? If it is true, then why don't we all just start loving each other? There is a disconnect somewhere between what we believe about love and the reality we experience, but we all seem to believe in love. Let me give you an example from the Bible: "If I speak in the tongues of men and of angels, but have not love, I am a noisy gong or a clanging cymbal. And if I have prophetic powers, and understand all mysteries and all knowledge, and if I have all faith, so as to remove mountains, but have not love, I am nothing. If I give away all I have, and if I deliver up my body to be burned, but have not love, I gain nothing" (1 Corinthians 13:1–3).

When you read this, do you not go, "Yes!"? The Bible is saying that it does not matter what you have in life if you do not have love. Love is what we need! But why is it that we feel this way? Why is it that deep down, we long to connect with people, to be known by people, to have relationships with people? Here is the reality: Most people who speak about love really mean feeling in love. The love of a friend, romantic love, and even sexual love are superior to any other feelings, but they never take it further than that. You cannot say love is ultimate unless you know how to trace that back to something ultimate. You cannot say, "Love is what we need," unless you can work backwards and show why we need love more than we need anything else. Why do we love? Why do we desire love? Why do we want love? Those are spiritual questions.

How do you know they are spiritual questions? Because all humans have asked them from the beginning of time until now. We can also tell that these questions are spiritual because other ways of thinking about them are insufficient. Sit down sometime with an evolutionary biologist and ask them to explain why we love from a biological perspective. The best answer they have is to connect love to sexual reproduction: "We love because we have to reproduce." What if you asked about friend love? "We love because long ago, our evolutionary ancestors had to stay together. If we stayed together, we survived, so we learned to combine a feeling with that and to connect it with love." That is an insufficient answer. How do you know it is insufficient?

Well, have you ever been in love? Not only romantic love, but have you ever had a friend who was there for you? Are you close to your family? Biology is not equipped to answer to fully explain those realities. If you are a biologist, I am not blaming you. Biology as a scientific field is great, but it is not equipped to explain why we love. No other worldview is, apart from the Bible.

It does not matter where you go for answers, to an atheistic worldview or to a theistic worldview; if you go to any other religion, you will find that the world began with one thing—power. What is God's primary relationship to the world? It is always one of creator to created. That is a relationship of power. If you create something, you have power over it. The primary problem with our ways of thinking about the world is the fact that love is not ultimate; power is ultimate. If you were to sit down with a Muslim and talk to them about who God is, they would not use words like "relationship." That is not primarily the way they interact with God. The concept of a relationship with God is not significant within Islam: God is God and you are not God; it is a relationship of power.

The dynamic of power is true in naturalism, too. If you believe in survival of the fittest, then you believe that we relate to each other primarily on the basis of power. We will gain power over each other, hold on to that power over each other, and then leverage that power for ourselves. Why do we relate to each other based on power? Because we believe that in the beginning, there was only power.

Only Christianity says that in the beginning there was love. In the first three verse of Genesis, we see there is something unique about the Christian God. We see the doctrine of the Trinity—one God in three persons. The Trinity is essential to Christianity because it shows us that in the beginning, there was love. Right off the bat, you can see all three persons of the Trinity. Verse one: "In the beginning, God created..." Here we have God the Father, God the Creator. This is the idea of God that many people have. Then verse two says, "and the Spirit of God was hovering over the face of the deep." Already, there is a distinction between God the Father and the Spirit of God. That word "hovering" implies a mother bird hovering over the nest. Even in the word "hovering," there is love language. So we have God the Father and God the Spirit, and then Moses wrote verse three: "And God said, let there be light, and there was light."

What are we to make of God's speaking? In John 1, we are told, "In the beginning was the word, the word was with God, and the word was God" (John 1:1). Who is the word? Jesus Christ. If we asked most Christians, "How did God create the world?" they would say, "By speaking it." But this speaking is a metaphor implying Jesus. This is what John is telling us in his gospel.

Three verses into Genesis, we have God the Father, God the Son, God the Spirit. You can see this dynamic again in verse 26 of chapter 1: "Then God said, 'let us make man in our image, after our likeness.'". Do you hear the plural language? Certainly, atheism cannot hear it, and any other kind of theism cannot hear it. Only Christianity says that in the beginning, God said things like "we" and "us" and "our."

Why is this significant? This means that before the foundation of the world, there was God, relating to himself. There was not just God going, "Let there be a world." Rather, there was God the Father loving God the Son, and God the Son loving God the Spirit, and going around and around. This means that in Christianity, God is primarily love first, and then power. It means that God's power is the overflow of his love—love first, because before God did anything, he loved. Then he created. What is love primarily? What is power? It is an instrument of love. If, in the beginning, God is love, then everything God does flows out of that love. When God says, "Let there be light," when he makes people, when he makes animals, when he makes the land, the garden, and when he shapes it and he puts them in it, this is all the overflow of love.

Before the beginning of the world, the triune God existed as Father, Son, and Spirit—existing as three persons, yet one essence. Before there was an earth, before there was a cosmos, before there was anything, there was the triune God existing in this circular relationship between each person of the Godhead. He is perfectly happy, perfectly content, and perfectly together. When God creates, what is the purpose of creation? What is the purpose of making people? Why is God speaking with them and walking in the garden with them? He is increasing the circle. This is how God made the world; he enlarged the circle. Adam and Eve were in paradise because they were in the circle of God's love.

C. S. Lewis said, "All sorts of people are fond of repeating the statement that God is love, but they seem not to notice that the words God is love have no real meaning unless God contains at least two persons. Love is something that one person has for another person. If God was a single person, then before the world was made, he was not love, and that by the way is perhaps the most important different between Christianity and all other religions. That in Christianity God is not a static thing, but a dynamic pulsating activity, a life almost a kind of drama, almost if you will, not think me irreverent, a kind of dance."

Only Christianity says before the world began, there was love. Only Genesis says before the world began, there was love. Moving forward to the Gospels, God the Father speaks one time. What does he say? "This is my beloved Son, with whom I am well pleased" (Matthew 3:17). And when Jesus talks, who does he talk about? God the Father. When Jesus tells his disciples the Holy Spirit is coming, what is the Holy Spirit going to talk about? Jesus! This is the circle, this is the dance C. S. Lewis is describing. Though many say love is ultimate, only the Christian can say that before there was anything, there was love, and God is primarily love.

The answer to what we're looking for, fixing the world with love, has to be traced back to something, and we can only trace it back to the God who is love. If we dive into the rest of Genesis and say, "What is this 'day' nonsense? As modern people, we can't believe that," then we have already missed the point. God has revealed to us through Moses the foundations of our desire for love and we want to talk about matter? When we lie in bed at night, do we miss matter or do we miss love? We miss love. Why is it that we say, "I want love above all things"? Why is it that people will throw everything away for love? Why is it that poor people with love are happier than rich people without it? Why do we write about love, sing about love, and paint about love? The Bible tells us that inherent in all of us is a trace memory of love. When God created us, he was walking in a circle with himself, joyfully, and he invited us into the circle. He brought Adam and Eve into the circle, and they were all walking around. This is life: knowing God, loving God, and being brought into eternity through fellowship with God. The whole universe is the overflow of an eternal relationship between one God in three persons.

But the fellowship between humans and God did not last. We sinned against God and we eliminated ourselves from the circle, so the circle closed up—yet when we lie in bed at night, we have a trace memory of what it means to be loved and how only love will satisfy us. We don't know all that we miss, but we miss something. The Bible says we miss the love of God. Because love is primary. This answer is complete in a way that no other answer is. No other worldview provides this. To reduce our answers down to biology and physics is really ridiculous. Why do we dance in our hearts and our minds to a relational rhythm? Because the God who is ultimately love and relationship created us.

The Artistic Rhythm

Human beings are hardwired to want meaning. Even among atheistic, naturalist thinkers of our day, there is a real conversation going on about why we think and want and feel, why we are conscious creatures. If you see a lion lying under a tree looking at you, you know he is not pondering existential questions. But why do we hunger for meaning? Why do we want? Why do we create art?

Why do we enjoy the kinds of paintings, books, songs, or poems that shock us to our very core? We know when we are in the presence of great art, when we are in the presence of something otherworldly. If you have ever been in front of great art, you know that. I am not talking about some forms of art that fade away. I am talking about art that lasts. When you're in the presence of art, you know it. Why? In what way are we intersecting with something bigger than ourselves? What is the bigger thing we long to belong to? Look at the first verse of Genesis to find the answer. Moses writes, "In the beginning ..." (Genesis 1:1a). "In the beginning" is story language. It is narrative language. Moses is saying that in the moment of creation, a story began and it is ongoing. The reason we long for meaning, the reason we long for great art, the reason it lasts centuries is that it is tapping into a larger existential reality. It taps into the story that we are a part of. The Bible says that story is the story of God shaping human history. The Bible does not begin with human history, work backwards, and then try to interpret it. It is not a commentary on history. The Bible begins at creation and says, "This is why there even is human history."

We all know there is a universe. "Where did it come from?" is not the best question. The better question we need answered is "Why is there a universe?" The Bible says there is a universe because God is writing a cosmic story. We long for meaning because we are meant to be part of that story.

God does not live on the Earth. He created a garden, put people in it, and said, in essence, "This is how the story unfolds." And when we stand in front of great art or listen to great music and say, "This is something bigger than right now. This is some other kind of reality. This is some other kind of world," these are little snippets of divine moments where God is whispering, "You are right. You are a part of a greater story, and you are right to want to be a part of that."

When you were young, you were probably told you were a unique snowflake. Then, by the time you hit twenty, people keep telling you that you are less like a snowflake than you used to be. Coming to this realization feels empty and no good. But have you ever moved beyond yourself and been a part of something huge? Do you remember how great that feeling was? That feeling was just a shadow of what it feels like to take our place in God's story of human history. When you ask, "Why?" the Bible has answers. Because God is writing a great story.

The Mechanical Rhythm.

It is not enough to know that there is a story. We must have a place in the story. We need purpose. If the artistic rhythm of the heart corresponds to meaning, then the mechanical rhythm corresponds to purpose. After Moses says, "In the beginning, God created the heavens and the earth," he then says that "the Earth was formless and void." The land was uninhabitable wilderness. Who does Moses have in mind when he says the world was a chaotic, uninhabitable wilderness? He is thinking of humans who are going to live on the land.

Land is a prominent theme in the Pentateuch. God took his people to the promised land. Once they got in the land, things would go well, but in the beginning, that land was uninhabitable. Thankfully, it could not stay that way, because God was writing a story and we had a place in that story. We needed a place to live if we were going to be part of the story.

Envision God as a great novelist writing a great novel and creating characters who fit into the story. These characters will move the story forward, but the story is ultimate, not the characters. Each character plays a role in this story, but the story is God's to write and shape. We can use Moses as an example. When Deuteronomy ends, Moses dies and God's people are going into the promised land without him. Moses is important, but he is not ultimate. The story is ultimate. Moses rises and Moses falls, but regardless, the story keeps moving. If we are all unique snowflakes, then the stories rise and fall with us, but if we are a part of something bigger, the story always rises and it never falls with us.

Why do we want love? Why do we want meaning? Why do we want purpose? It is because we were created for love. It is because God is love. It is because love is primary. It is because we have a trace memory, an ancestral memory of walking in a circle with God and we want that back. Other kinds of love are just shadows of that divine love. This is why we stand in front of a great painting in awe. This is why we lie in bed at night saying, "I wish I was part of something bigger than me," and God whispers, "You were meant to be."

These plotlines start at the beginning. That means there is going to be a middle, a climax, and an ending. That means we are going somewhere. There is a trajectory to human history.

We could sum the Bible up this way: The Bible is an argument for what it means to be human. The Bible says you will never really come alive until you discover the purpose you have in the meaning motivated by love. When we accept these answers deep down in our souls, in places where biology, physics, and chemistry do not reach, we know it is true.

How do we know this is true? Because two thousand years ago, God became a man. He was a man who elevated love above all things. He was not a man who simply went around speaking of love, saying things like "Let us just love each other." He was a man who did it. Even when religious folks would defy him, saying things like "You can't do that on the Sabbath," he chose love. Even when people hated him, he chose love. Not only did he choose love, he talked a lot about meaning. He talked about how God was doing something. He described how long ago, God said he would come to rescue his people. He told us what would happen to him in this life, how he would die, and what would happen after he died. Jesus also understood his purpose in God's story. He told his disciples that he came for this purpose: "The Son of Man came not to be served but to serve, love, and to give his life as a ransom for many" (Mark 10:45).

Love, meaning, and purpose: For these, the Son of Man came. What did Jesus mean when he said he came? Well, we didn't come to earth; we were born. We didn't have a choice, but Jesus said he had a choice and he chose to come to us. Why did he come? He came to serve. Jesus said that power is not ultimate. Love is ultimate, and Jesus's ultimate purpose was to give his life as a ransom for many.

Only one man lived this love, meaning, and purpose to perfection, and he changed the world. We are still talking about him over two thousand years later. He is the key that unlocks the whole Bible. The Bible is God's story, and Jesus is the central character. Without him, the story makes no sense. He lived a life of love, meaning, and purpose to accomplish two things. First, he wanted to show us what would happen if we lived like that. When you read the Gospels, you will have that moment of awe when the life of Jesus hits you in the face and you say, "Yes! This is life! This is what I am looking for! This is what physical things can't answer! This is what it means to love, and live, and have meaning!" Then you also will find that he says he came for us. He opened the circle of God's love back up.

On the cross, where Jesus died, he who had always known the circle of perfect fellowship with God stepped out of the circle. What does Jesus cry on the cross? "My God, My God, why have you forsaken me?" (Matthew 27:46). This cry is outside the circle language. For the first time in the history of the world, a member of the Godhead had an outside-the-circle experience. He left the circle in order to grab people and bring them back into fellowship with God.

It is only inside this circle that we will find the love, meaning, and purpose we are looking for. Would we not agree, before we worry ourselves with physical things, there are larger questions? To the larger questions, there are larger answers, and Jesus answers them all.

Chapter 2

Man or Machine

Genesis 1:26–2:17

When Moses was writing and assembling the Pentateuch, the first five books of the Bible, he had a specific goal in mind: to remind the Israelites, as they got ready to cross into the promised land, of the answer to the metaphysical questions that humanity has always asked—questions like "Who is God?"; "Who are we?"; and "What's our purpose?" As we discussed previously, Moses is not primarily interested in physical things, although much of our contemporary conversation about Genesis tends to center around those physical things. Moses is primarily interested in addressing foundational spiritual questions. Because the book is an argument, Moses is not writing in a vacuum. He's not under the delusion that as Israel goes into the promised land, its view will be the only view. He understands the promised land is a place of religious pluralism. It's a place where there will be many ideas about who God is and who we are. Moses is writing to combat them.

In the same way Moses wrote to combat the pluralism of his world, Genesis and the Pentateuch as a whole can be read as an argument over and against the worldviews of our culture. Today, many assume science and the Bible are disagreeing over questions like "Who is man?"; "What is humanity?"; and "What does it mean to be human?" Regarding these questions, true science and Christianity don't actually disagree. Instead, we take science, which is designed to answer only the physical, and we seek to raise it up to answer the metaphysical. When this happens, naturalism and materialism are formed as worldviews and we prop up science to do something it was never designed to do. When we do this, we end up with answers that are very different than the Bible. Much of the thinking in our culture would present humanity as a machine, the result of a process of random scientific things happening to you as an organism. You are simply the result of those things. This thinking is the exact opposite of what the Bible says.

What does it really mean to be human? Moses answers this question in four points in the book of Genesis: relationship, role, rule, and rest.

Relationship

Throughout the creation narrative, we see that humanity enjoys a special relationship with God. First, God consults with himself when it's time to make people. Look at Genesis 1:26; God says, "Let us make man in our image after our likeness." As we've discovered reading the beginning of Genesis 1, we find that the triune God is present. In Genesis 1:1, Moses writes, "In the beginning, God created the heavens and the earth." In Genesis 1:2, Moses describes the Spirit of God hovering above the waters. In Genesis 1:3, we see God creating through the word, which the Gospel of John tells us is Jesus, the Son. The triune God is all over creation, and yet no conversation takes place until verse 26. God the Father is speaking things the entire time, but you notice a pause when we get to verse 26. The action slows down and God says, "Let's have a Trinity huddle here. Let's talk amongst ourselves and let's create something in our own image. Let's make man in our own image." Now, here's our working definition of "image of God." Whatever is true of humans that is not true of animals is what it means to be made in the image of God.

Notice two things in the text. First, notice that there's a pause in the action. Then notice that God's special relationship with humanity begins as God consults with himself as he makes people. We will see in Genesis 2 that God gets literally dirty when he makes people. God is what you would call upper management. Upper management doesn't get dirty. We go from a speaking God who "let there be this and let there be that" to a God actually getting down in the dirt and forming something. Read the words of Moses: "Then the Lord God formed the man from dust in the ground. And breathed into his nostrils the breath of life. And the man became a living creature" (Genesis 2:7). There's necessarily no difference between God saying, "Let there be a man," and God saying, "Let me form a man," in the sense that God is the creator either way. God is no less the creator of the sun than he is of humans, even though he didn't form the sun from dust. He just said, "Let there be lights in the expanse of heaven," (Genesis 1:14). So why is it important that we know that God got down on his knees and formed humanity? It is important because it describes intimacy. Here you have God not simply speaking but actually putting man together. This is fundamentally why Christians say, "Everything in the universe is good. Dogs, for example, are good. But dogs are not as valuable as people." If you ask, "Why is that true?" the answer is because God spoke animals into existence but he got down in the dirt to make people.

If you read Genesis chapters 1 and 2, you'll see that everything God does is to create an environment where people can flourish. It's similar to when a woman is about seven months into a pregnancy; she enters into the nesting phase. Everything in the house gets rearranged and put back together in the way she sees fit. The mother is getting the home ready to be a place where children can flourish. When you read Genesis 1 and 2, you see that God is nesting. He is making a place for humanity to flourish. In Genesis 1, every time God creates, Moses has written, "and God said." Ten times, Moses used the word "and," but when he gets to the creation of man, Moses writes, "*then* God said." What's the distinction there? All the "ands" were just to get us to the "then." It would be like saying, "We went home, and we moved this table, and we put the plastic things in the light sockets, and we baby-proofed our drawers, and we put the crib together. Then the baby came." That's what's going on here. God has created a universe; he's created an earth for humanity to flourish on.

We also know the earth is designed for humanity when God says, "Fill the earth and subdue it, and have dominion." (Genesis 1:28b)—in other words, "Let them have control." Moses understands that everything created is for man to flourish. Why are there plants? They are for man to eat and grow and build things. Why are there animals? They are for man to take care of and cultivate and domesticate and do all these other things. Why is there dirt? So we can walk on it. Why is there a sky? So we can breathe. Why are there all these things? It's for people. By the way, this explanation is not contra-science. This is actually right in line with science. Physicists marvel today at how fine-tuned our universe is for human life: Just a little tweak here, just a little change there; if the dial were just a little turned, humans couldn't survive. Why are all the dials turned directly to where they need to be? The Bible says it's because God created the world for people.

Look at what Moses has written in chapter 2: "And the Lord God planted a garden in Eden in the East and there he put man whom he had formed and out of the ground the Lord God made to spring up every tree that is pleasant to the sight and good for food" (Genesis 2:8–9a). Sometimes, if you haven't grown up in church, you come in with this idea that the garden of Eden was this otherworldly paradise and it's this mystical place. Humans got to be there and then they got kicked out, but nobody knows where it is. But Moses gave us the geography. The garden of Eden was idyllic not because it was mystical but rather because it was the place God created for Adam and Eve to flourish in. The emphasis in Genesis 2 is not on the garden; it's on Adam and Eve. God creates a garden and puts man in the garden. When he creates people, he takes them, he places them, and it's as if he says, "Stay here. This is best for you." See the nesting imagery here? Adam and Eve weren't in the garden by accident.

God also gives humanity choice. He doesn't give this concept of making conscious choices to anyone else, but to the humans, he says, "You may surely eat of every tree of the garden. But of the tree of the knowledge of good and evil you shall not eat. For in that day, the day you eat of it, you will surely die" (Genesis 2:16). What's the implication? By God creating a tree and telling his creation not to eat of it, he's allowing the possibility of them eating it. Why? You cannot have a real relationship unless you have vulnerability. God is whispering to Adam and Eve, "The plants do what I tell them to do because I've created this thing called photosynthesis. The animals do what I've told them to do because I've created this ecological cycle. But you must choose to do what I've created you to do. I have a relationship with the plants, but it's one as natural-law maker and natural-law follower. I have a relationship with the animals, but it's the same as with the plants. With you, it's creator and created. It's God and man."

Lastly, we know that humans have a special relationship with God because he puts this status on all people at all times. In the beginning, there's only Adam and Eve, yet God doesn't say, "If you have children, they don't get this." He is saying, "This is what it means to be human. You have relationship with me. You're made in my image. I got dirty when I made you. I created the world as a place for you to flourish. And I've given you a choice. This status is on all people, all times, all places, all ethnicities; all kinds of people get this kind of status." So what does it mean to be human? Our first answer is that it means to enjoy a unique and special relationship with God, because you're made in his image, because he's created the world as a place for you to thrive. This is important because it tells us two things.

First, to be human is to be known and loved by God. Our relationship with God is the shout that all other relationships echo. To be in a great relationship, you need to be known and loved. The problem is that in most of our relationships, we're either known and not loved because they know us, or we're loved and not known. They may think we're great, but they don't know us that well. It's very rare that we stumble into a relationship in which we are known and loved. In fact, if you're in a relationship in which you're loved and not known, the most terrifying thing to you is for this person to truly know you. The scariest thing to any of us is others knowing us and then rejecting us. The Bible says any great relationship is the residue of a relationship with God from the beginning, when we were known and loved.

It also shows us that all human life has value. If naturalism is correct and we are simply the result of chemistry and biology, we're simply the end product of a random process, and life, death, and reality are a mirage, just a construct to help us make sense of the world. If you buy into thinking that we are simply the result of scientific, physical processes, then you are not far from the thinking of one prominent academic who says that if a person is under the age of two, over the age when they're no longer able to live on their own, or mentally handicapped, society ought to be able to put them down because they do not provide value. It's the end result of naturalist thinking. The Bible says your healthy child and your mentally handicapped child have the same value because they're both made in the image of God. We intrinsically know this. That's why when we hear the news of somebody walking into a mall and shooting people, we say, "Oh my goodness, that's awful!" Why? Because people are made in the image of God. Because humans enjoy a special relationship with God.

Role

Humans not only enjoy a special relationship with God but also have a specific role with God. So if we agree with Genesis 1, that the world was created for humans to flourish on, then the goodness of creation must be interpreted through the lens of what's good for humanity. Moses wrote to end chapter 1, "God saw everything he had made and behold it was very good and there was evening and there was morning, the sixth day" (Genesis 1:31).

Why was it good? It was good because it was good for people. He creates man, and after this, everything is good. We've got the whole system, and man is over everything. We have the animals, plants, and earth all under man. The world was created for humanity, so the goodness of the world is filtered through the lens of humanity.

Genesis 2:10–14 is an example of a passage in the Bible that we can read and skip over. Why should we care about rivers and waters? Number one, because water happens to be the life source of humanity, particularly in an agricultural society. You've got to have water. Moses writes that the garden of Eden has rivers. Why is that important? The rivers water the ground. Why is this important? Because humans need water. Why is Moses telling us there was water and gold and stones? Because humans care about those things, because we use them, because we shape and mold them. This is further evidence that the garden of Eden was designed for humans.

At the beginning of Genesis 2, God rests and he gives the baton to humanity. Moses writes, "And on the seventh day, God finished his work that he had done and he rested on the seventh day from all his work that he had done" (Genesis 2:2). The seventh day doesn't have an end. All the other days have ends. God is in a permanent state of rest, but we must not confuse rest with inactivity. This is not a deistic view of God who creates the world and then steps away and says, "Don't screw it up." Instead, God's rest is a feeling of contentment. It's as if God is saying all the necessary work is done. If we combine God resting with what he says at the end of chapter 1—"And God blessed them and God said to them 'Be fruitful and multiply and fill the earth and subdue it and have dominion over every living thing that moves on the Earth'"—God is essentially saying to humanity, "I've made a world is now you shape it! Mold it! Cultivate it! Mine it! Build things on it! Create culture! Make music! Paint paintings! Make babies! Do all of those things." The Bible says that it's a good world and God gives it to us and tells us to go make something out of it. The whole universe is set up for us to discover it.

Science is a large part of the cultural mandate that God gives Adam and Eve. God tells us to subdue the earth. How do you subdue it? You subdue it by observing it, seeing how things work, coming up with systems and imposing them on the land. That's science. God also talks about cultivating. What is that? That's art through culture creation. God gave us stuff. We discover the stuff. We shape it, mold it, and create culture, art, science. That's what it means to be human.

This logic means things for us as humans. It means that God is neither an ultra-environmentalist nor whatever the opposite of whatever you would call an anti-environmentalist. In American politics, the left wing says to cut a tree down is the equivalent of cutting a human down. God says that is clearly not true. We are to mold and shape with our dominion. The right wing says trees are just here for us to have anyways. The Bible says not true, because Adam and Eve are to cultivate and keep the garden. They are to subdue the earth and have dominion over it. They are also caretakers. God is telling us to take care of the earth but also have dominion over the earth. Whatever work we find to do is a part of the design of God. Work comes before sin, and it is good. Work is shaping and cultivating and providing. Work is taking the earth and making it a livable place; therefore, all work has meaning. Christianity says to run your own company is great and to be the janitor is great. Work is inherently good. It's part of what it means to be human. The CEO has no more value than the janitor.

When God creates the world, he places humanity between him and the world. The order is God, then humans, and then the world. If you're a deer and you want to get to God, you've got to go to humans. God has given Adam the responsibility so that when the world relates to God, it relates to God through Adam, who is the regional supervisor over all of God's creation. This is what it means to be human.

What else does this mean for us? It means that you cannot separate humans from purpose and meaning. When you go to bed at night and you think, *It just feels like my life has no meaning,* that absence is there because there was this reality in the beginning. You were created for meaning. If you were simply the product of biochemistry, you wouldn't have any meaning, other than to maybe keep your species going. What ultimate difference would that make? If your species dies out, you're not going to be around to notice. It's the Bible that says humans have purpose and meaning. It's the Bible that says this is our earth to shape and cultivate. That means if you're not a Christian and you say, "I'm for the environment! We have to save the rainforests!" you say it because deep in your heart, you feel the residue of what God has designed you to do.

Rule

To be human is also to be under God's rule. Even though Adam and, eventually, Eve are over the garden, God is over them. The Bible says, "The Lord God took the man and put him in the garden" (Genesis 2:15). God picks up Adam and says something like "Here you go. This is your home." In this interaction, there is an inherent relationship between God, the creator, and Adam, the created. This is why God puts the tree of the knowledge of good and evil in the garden. The tree is to remind Adam every day that he is a created thing and not the creator. God says, "You may surely eat of every tree in the garden. But of the tree of the knowledge of good and evil you shall not eat" (Genesis 2:16). So why the tree of the knowledge of good and evil? Why name it that? God is saying, "Listen, Adam, you're going to flourish as long as you remember that you depend on me for your understanding of the world. As long as you trust me to tell you what's good and bad, as long as you listen to me, as long as you depend on me and my vision and my understanding, you're going to be great. You're going to flourish. You're going to thrive. I've been nesting. I've created this wonderful world for you. But when you start to think that you are the creator, not the created, that's when there's going to be trouble." That's what's going on here. Why the tree? Adam is conscious. He has choice. God's saying to Adam, "Here's the tree. Every day you walk past this tree and don't eat, you are worshipping the creator, saying, 'What a great privilege it is to live as a created thing in a created universe!' On the day you eat of the tree, you will break our relationship. You'll be out from under my rule, and that won't be good for you."

Here's the implication: God equates human submission with human thriving. This is fundamental to all of Christianity. God says that we will thrive and we will flourish when we are under his rule. Fundamentally behind the law of God, behind the rule of God, is the desire for humans to flourish. Submission is not designed to restrict human flourishing, but to enhance it. Why is the relationship between submission and flourishing important? It's important because we believe that human flourishing lies outside the rule of God. We believe that the rule of God imposes restrictions on us; however, the essence of God's law is human flourishing.

Rest

What is the result of all these things? The result is rest "And on the seventh day, God finished the work that he had done. And God rested on the seventh day from all the work that he had done" (Genesis 2:2). If God's at rest, the whole world's at rest. If God says the work is done, the work is done. God says the ultimate work is done and the only work left to do is to discover, to create, to shape, to mold. When you're doing those kinds of things, you never feel like you're working. True rest is not relaxation. We can tell ourselves, "I will only be at rest when I'm at the beach with a drink in my hand," but when you're working on something great, what do you feel? You feel rested. Why? Because you were created to do it. Humans in relationship with God, fulfilling their role, under his rule, will be people who rest.

What does it mean to be human? God answers: It is to be in perfect relationship with him. To be known by him and loved by him. It is to fulfill a specific role. It is to shape if you're a shaper, and to cultivate if you're a creator. Finally, it means to be under his authority. When you do that, you'll find you're resting. What a great definition of what it means to be human!

That may be what it *means* to be human, but is this our *experience* of being human? Do I know God, personally? Do I know him more than the plant knows him? Do I know him more than the animal knows him? Am I serving him in a specific role with a specific purpose? Do I go to work understanding that my work and my performance are linked to what God is doing in the world? And, ultimately, do I submit to his authority? Do I say, "How does God define love? How does God define trust? How does God define work? How does God define sex?" Or am I seeking to define those things myself? The answer is that all of us, maybe on all points, often fall short. Primarily, we are people who are not at rest. God is saying there's a mathematical relationship here: Relationship plus role plus rule equals rest. When we remove one of those pieces from the equation, we don't get rest. What are we to do?

Moses leaves us a little clue here in this passage. He is not writing from the garden of Eden. He is standing in Moab, outside the promised land, having seen people die and having seen his fellow Hebrews as slaves in Egypt. He knows the world as we know the world. He knows it as a fallen, broken, restless place, and here's what he says: "So God blessed the seventh day and made it holy because on it God rested from all his work that he had done in creation" (Genesis 2:3). He's talking about the Jewish practice of the Sabbath. Why is the Sabbath important? Because the Sabbath reminds people of the rest of God created for the world—the rest of shalom, peace, and settledness. The point of the Sabbath is spiritual, not physical. God is telling Adam, in essence, "You rest from your work to be reminded that I have done all the work that is necessary and you're simply shapers and cultivators." What do we tell ourselves? We tell ourselves the universe depends on us, my universe depends on me. The Sabbath is a pause button to say, "Your universe does not depend on you. Your universe has never depended on you. It has always depended on God." The problem is that the Sabbath is one day a week, and not a life of rest.

Today, you can go to church and get fired up about God and your role shaping and cultivating, but then you get into Monday and it goes straight downhill. One day a week doesn't fix us, so the Sabbath is simultaneously a celebration and also an anvil around our necks, because on the Sabbath, you'd say things like "Why can't every day be like this?" and "Why aren't I like this?" The answers are found in Genesis 3 when Adam and Eve eat from the tree, when Adam and Eve say, "Human flourishing is outside God's authority, not inside." One day a week is not a world at rest after this.

In the New Testament, the writer of Hebrews tells us in chapter 4 that there is a greater rest to which the Sabbath points: the rest that comes through Jesus Christ. In the Gospels, Jesus says, "Come to me, all who labor and are heavy laden, and I will give you rest" (Matthew 11:28). How can he say that? Because he is, in his own words, the Lord of the Sabbath (Matthew 12:8). He is a living, breathing Sabbath. This is a man who traveled all the time. This is a man who healed people until every sick person was healed. He knows how exhausting it is. He is implying, "Come to me, and although you work, I'll realign your work. I'll reconnect you to God. Your relationship and your work under God's rule will put you at rest." Jesus also said, "My yoke is easy and my burden is light" (Matthew 11:30). He said that on the way to the cross. Why? Because Jesus Christ was the only man in the history of the world who lived perfectly in relationship with God, fulfilling his role under God's rule. Remember what he prays in the garden: "My Father, if it be possible, let this cup pass from me; nevertheless, not as I will, but as you will" (Matthew 26:39)? In other words, "I don't really want to do this, but not what I want, God, but what you want. God, I don't necessarily feel that this is the way to human flourishing, particularly my own, but I'll trust you to define human flourishing."

Jesus Christ, the only man to have ever lived perfectly in relationship, perfectly fulfilling his role, perfectly under God's rule, was sacrificed on the cross willingly. Why? So that the world could be put back together. He who had always trusted God for good and evil was punished as one who had eaten from the tree of good and evil in order that you and I might be brought back into rest. How can we know God? Only through Jesus, who said, "Whoever has seen me has seen the Father" (John 14:9). How can I know God? Only through Jesus. How can I find my role? How can I find my purpose? Only in knowing God, so only through Jesus. How can I be brought back under God's rule? You can leave today and say, "I'm going to do only what God tells me to do because my preacher said that means I'm going to flourish," but you'll fail, and even if you could do it perfectly from here on out, you've already failed. Your only hope is to look to Jesus, who, in the garden, said what you and I never say: "Not as I will, but as you will" (Matthew 26:39). He said it for our benefit.

If you say, "I don't feel rested," you've got to turn to Jesus. If you say, "But I've turned to Jesus. I don't feel rested," you've got to turn back to Jesus. You've got to stop believing the lie that your work will give you status. It won't. Only Jesus will. You can't earn status. You've got to stop believing the lie that your own flourishing comes outside God's love. You've got to look to Jesus, who provides all these things for us.

Chapter 3

Power, Pleasure, or Purpose?

Genesis 2:18-25

The Bible starts with the following premise: God is good and loving, and he wants us to flourish. He wants us to be successful and to make progress. This is important because the way in which we engage God is influenced by how we understand God. In Genesis 2:18–25, God zooms in on this concept of human flourishing with the ideas of gender, marriage, and sex. The Bible argues for us to view the world, gender, marriage, and sex according to God's design. These are indispensable parts for God's plan for humanity. They are essential. This matters for us because every human has a gender, many are married or will seek marriage, all think about sex, and, finally, our culture disagrees with the biblical view of gender, marriage, and sex in just about every way possible.

As we have discussed, Genesis is primarily an argument. Moses has not written just to write. Israel is getting ready to cross into the promised land, and he knows when they get there, they are going to encounter all kinds of worldviews, so in the first five books of the

Bible, the Pentateuch, he is basically making an argument for who God is, who the Israelites are, and how they should interact with God. They should trust him. More specifically, they should listen to him on things like gender, marriage, and sex.

When you are evaluating worldviews, you should ask yourself which worldview has the best explanatory power. Which one can explain the things that we know and the things that we experience? Which one can answer the questions that we ask?

What Is Gender?

Gender is an essential part of what it means to be human. Genesis 1:26 says, "Let us make man in our image." And then Moses writes in verse 27, "So God created man in his image. In the image of God he created him. Male and female he created him." From the very first mention of humanity in the Bible, there is no reference to humanity apart from the reference to gender. Gender is an essential part of what it means to be human. This is over and against some in our culture who argue that gender is a social construct imposed by society. That thinking is opposite what the Bible says. The Bible says that from the very beginning, there was gender; there were males and there were females. In fact, the idea that gender is irrelevant is not only opposite the biblical worldview but also opposite most feminist arguments. Many people credit Carol Gilligan's book from 1982, *In a Different Voice*, as being a seminal moment in the feminist movement. In this book, Gilligan argues that psychology has steered us wrong in many ways because psychology made observations of men and then made those observations universal. Psychologists were looking at men and women and saying essentially, "This is true of men, so therefore it is true of all people," and Carol Gilligan, a feminist, says in the book that that presumption is not true. She points out that men and women differ in all essential ways, including their psychological development, moral reasoning, and motivations. The thesis of the book, Gilligan says, is that men seek maturity through detachment and women seek maturity through attachment. And that nuanced difference is fundamental to understanding what it means to be human.

You cannot look at humanity and say, "What is male and female? We are all human!" That is wrong, according to Carol Gilligan, according to feminism, and according to the Bible. It is wrong to say men and women are the same. We are not the same. We are different, and the differences are important. They are essential to what it means to be human.

Gender is also essential to what it means to be made in the image of God. Genesis 1:26–27 says, "Let us make man in our image, so God created man in his own image. In the image of God he created him. Male and female he created them." The maleness of males and the femaleness of females both display the image of God because we are not similar, but rather we are made in particular ways; therefore, you can say that women image God in ways men do not, and men image God in ways that women do not. Some people say, "Gender is a peripheral Christian thing. It is not essential." The Bible says that gender is essential because the image of God is essential. Gender helps us display the image of God because the Bible teaches there is one God in three persons. In the beginning there was love and there was relationship. You had one God in three persons relating to himself, so when God said, "We have to make man in our image," he realized he could not do that through one gender. He must create a nuanced difference—a difference of role and of function so that humanity can dance, just like the triune God has been dancing since eternity past.

Gender is a precise tool in the fulfillment of the mandate that God gives humanity. God blesses humanity and says, "Be fruitful and multiply and fill the earth and subdue it and have dominion over the fish of the sea and over the birds in the heavens and over every living thing that moves on the earth" (Genesis 1:28). What a job! God says to humanity, "I am going to rest. You shape, you mold, and you work." In Genesis Chapter 2, he takes Adam and Eve and he places them in the garden and he says, "Work it and keep it" (Genesis 2:15b). God creates male and female and gives the mandate to both so that both men and women are uniquely equipped to participate in every piece of the mandate. God does not say in Genesis 1, "Men, you have dominion. Women, you multiply." He says to all people, men and women, masculine and feminine, that we have a mission to accomplish.

Some scholars critique Genesis and say it is similar to other creation mythologies. While the Bible borrows from some things, the Bible contains several things that other creation accounts do not. One uniqueness to Genesis is its separate, unique account of the creation of a woman. The Bible has this account of a woman being created to show that just as man is essential to the fulfillment of God's mission for humanity, so is woman. This is further shown when God brings the animals to Adam and every creature has a helper except Adam. Everything has been good until this point. The only time you see anything negative in the creation narrative is the absence of woman. God says, "It is not good that the man should be alone; I will make a helper fit for him" (Genesis 2:18b).

This shows that gender difference is born out of the intentional inadequacy of each gender. God looked at everything he had made and said it was good, except for what was intentionally not good. God is not saying Adam is lonely in Genesis 2:18. If God had said, "Adam is lonely," then it would mean God was inadequate. God is instead saying something like "I have given Adam this monster mission, and he will never accomplish it on his own." In fact, the Hebrew word here used for "helper" means literally "military reinforcements."

Reinforcements are given when a mission is not being accomplished. It is not good for Adam to be alone, because the mission is too big for him. God must send reinforcements. This is the same word often used to describe God in the Old Testament. God often comes to Israel's aid and tells them he will be their helper. God has not made Adam the kind of person to fulfill God's mission on his own, because God's design is for humanity to image him. Each member of the Godhead—Father, Son, and Holy Spirit—is interdependent with the others. In order for man to image God, man had to have an intentional interdependence.

This does not mean that God the Father, God the Son and God the Holy Spirit are inadequate. Their division of labor is intentional. Jesus submitted his life to the Father. He has all the authority the Father does, yet his labor is his willingness. As men and women, our labor is divided in our biology. God is saying, "This mission is too big for you and you will never image me on your own. You will image me and you will accomplish the mission when you have a helper—reinforcements." The idea here is not that Adam is strong and needs something pretty around the house, so he gets Eve. Instead, God is saying, "You have a big mission. I'm sending reinforcements. As you subdue, you will need her to help you. As you have dominion, you will need her to help you. As you are fruitful and multiply, you will need her to help you." There is a symbiosis here. There is a partnership, a collaboration, where both parties are absolutely fundamental. Eve is the only instance of troubleshooting in the garden. It is the only time God looks at something and says, "Not good" (Genesis 2:18a). Eve is the perfectly designed reinforcement for the mission of humanity.

Inherent in this passage is the idea of particular roles. In Genesis 2, Adam is given a mission and Eve is a helper. Helper does not mean "less than." It means as Adam subdues and as Adam takes dominion, Eve is involved in every piece of that. God is the head of the garden in Genesis, Adam is under him, and Eve is under Adam in her role, but not in equality. Gender differences matter, but Genesis 2 shows that men are not superior to women; women exist because men are inadequate.

In our culture, gender is a power issue, but in the Bible, it is a purpose issue. In our culture, the conversation about gender focuses on gaining power by asserting your gender's superiority. To be gendered is to assert yourself; you are asserting your dominance. Or our culture believes there are no gender distinctions; we are homogeneous beings. We either deal with gender by competing or by saying we are not fundamentally man or woman but are human and can figure out the gender stuff later—some of which society figures out for us, some of which we figure out. The Bible says the opposite. The Bible is saying the key to human flourishing is not male dominance or female dominance. The key to human flourishing is not pretending that gender does not exist. Instead, the key to human flourishing is both genders recognizing they have a role in the purpose of humanity, and collaborating together to fulfill that mission.

What Is Marriage?

Marriage is the primary mechanism for the dance of the genders. The dance of marriage is based on the dance of the Trinity. This is all over Genesis 2: "It is not good for man to be alone, I will make a helper fit for him" (Genesis 2:18). After declaring this, God brought the animals to the man to see what he would call them, but for Adam, there was not a helper fit for him (Genesis 2:19–21). Then, we see Adam singing a song: "This at last is bone of my bone and flesh of my flesh, she shall be called woman because she was taken out of man" (Genesis 2:23). Finally, God declares, "They shall become one flesh" (Genesis 2:24b). There's a lot of relational language here. There's a lot of dancing going on. Adam and Eve look at each other and say, in essence, "You fit me and I fit you and we complement each other and we have a divine mission." The natural result of the design of genders is a marriage. Marriage is like the canvas, and gender is like the paint. Marriage is the canvas on which the beauty of both genders is designed to shine and on which the genders work together to form a cohesive picture and mission. In fact, the Hebrew word here used for "fit" literally means "like opposite."

Eve is like opposite. She is human and she bears the image of God, yet she is opposite and unique. Eve's uniqueness is divinely instituted to come alongside Adam and to complete Adam. In the words of one commentator, "Each sex is gifted for different steps in the same great dance." That is a great way of saying it. In the beginning, there was man and woman. In the beginning, there was marriage because marriage is the mechanism by which gender will shine. You have God, then you have Adam as the leader of his home. Then you have Eve, the complementary reinforcement and the like opposite helper. Marriage is a lifetime commitment to embracing the other. When you are married and you say, "You drive me crazy!" Genesis 2 hints at this as if to say, "Exactly. That is because you are incomplete. That is because you are designed that way."

The roles are essential, but the way they flesh out in particular marriages is unique. This does not mean that the husband comes home, puts his feet up, grabs the remote. This does not mean that the wife cannot work. It does not mean that she cannot make more than her husband. God is saying there are absolute essential roles. It is not because the man has to have the checkbook or has to have the keys. That is a cultural, Western, American, male-dominating kind of thing. If you are a woman and you rebel against that, you are well to do so, but do not throw the baby out with the bathwater.

Marriage is also the primary mechanism for the cultural mandate given to humanity. When God says, "Be fruitful and multiply and fill the Earth and subdue it, and have dominion," he is expecting that the primary mechanism of realizing this mission is marriage (Genesis 1:28b). Be fruitful and multiply. In the Biblical worldview, this happens in the marriage. The family is an essential component of God's mission and mandate for humanity. Where do men and women learn best to collaborate together? The answer is marriage. It does not mean that what I do in my marriage is going to change the world, but it means that I will learn to embrace the other primarily through the mechanism of marriage in my own life. So many people delay marriage until they have everything figured out, but Genesis 2 is telling us we figure marriage out through being married! I am much more sensitive to women now than I was before I got married. By being married to a woman, I have learned how she thinks. I have learned to see the holes in my own thinking. I have learned the masculine response is not always the best response. I have learned the ways that I am stereotypically masculine and not Biblically masculine. She has exposed the weaknesses in me, lovingly, willingly, sometimes accidentally. That has made me into the kind of man who can better advance the human mission on this planet.

Our culture presents marriage as a source of pleasure. This gives a false view of reality and a predetermined expiration date. If you think marriage is about being happy, you are setting yourself up for failure. If you say to someone, "All I ask is that you make me happy for the rest of my life," that is a problem for two reasons. One, they cannot do that. Two, you cannot do that for them. It is funny how we ask of other people what we know we ourselves cannot give. There is so much divorce in America because we get married to make ourselves happy, and when pleasure and happiness are no longer in the marriage, or when we think someone else could give us more pleasure, we leave. The Bible says that marriage is not primarily about pleasure but about purpose, so that even in the moments where there is no happiness, it is exposing something in you. The fact that your spouse is like sandpaper rubbing against your rough edges is the point of marriage. Embrace that.

What is this saying about you? How is this showing your inadequacy? Serve your spouse by lovingly responding to them as they smooth out your edges. That is the design of marriage. I can run from my marriage and build a life where I can be selfish, or I can realize what is ultimate is to not be selfish. If married, we embrace our spouse and how they expose our selfishness. Many people avoid marriage because they are selfish to the core. If you get married, you can't stay selfish or you cannot stay married. One of those two. When you say, "I am not going to get married because life is about me," you are saying to God, "I will keep the paint, but I do not want your canvas."

Life is not about you. One of the greatest gifts of grace to teach you that is marriage. If you go into marriage thinking marriage will give you what only God will give you, it will absolutely destroy you. But if you go into marriage seeing it as a tool for God to give you what only God can give you, it will absolutely change you for the better.

What Is Sex?

Sex is an obvious biological part of the mandate given to humanity. You can't be fruitful and multiply without having sex. It's an obvious biological part of the cultural mandate. This is part and parcel of the Biblical view of children. Not only do some people not want to get married for selfish reasons, but equally grieving and equally opposed to the Biblical worldview is to get married and not want children. The primary reason we do not want children is because of selfishness. They get in the way of our careers, our money, and our weekends.

Part of what it is to be human is to have sex in order to biologically reproduce life. If you are a Christian, when you speak of marriage, you are called to speak of marriage in God's way. When you speak of children, you are called to speak of children in God's way and not in the culture's way. Some of you might be married and cannot have children. I mourn with you. But if you say, "I am going to get married and I am not going to have kids. I am going to live wherever I want. I am going to spend money however I want," the Bible says you have missed a foundational part of what it means to understand one of the roles of marriage. Marriage teaches us many things. One is that I have a heavenly Father who, no matter how many times I come to him, no matter how many times I am weak, no matter how many times I am wounded, no matter how many times I am needy, is there for me. And God the Father is telling us we will never truly understand what it means to image him until we can be there for someone else. And if we cannot be there for a twenty-month-old who is sick, we cannot be there for anybody. Do not run away from that. Do not trade that for a second car or a second garage or a second vacation. You will be giving up what is best for what is least.

Sex is also a part of the dance and a celebration of the one to whom the dance is pointing. Adam breaks out in the first R&B song in Genesis 2:23. You know what you're hearing there? You are hearing excitement. God brings animal after animal, and Adam goes, "No, no, no." Just when we think there is no hope, Adam takes a nap. He is emotionally exhausted. Then God makes the woman. Moses writes, "And the man and the wife were both naked and were not ashamed" (Genesis 2:25). That says so much in such a little sentence. There is a childlike innocence going on here. Adam and Eve see, love, know, and celebrate each other without shame or guilt. We come from a sexually conservative culture, but Moses is saying our own sexually conservative nature is a necessary result of sin. In the beginning, we were free, naked, and unashamed. If you get married and you have been sexually pure before marriage and even during marriage, there is an innocence there because there are no ghosts in the bedroom, there is nothing to compare the sexual part of your marriage to. Adam is looking at Eve and saying she is perfect. If Adam is looking at online pornography, then Eve stops being his definition of perfect. If Adam is looking at his coworker, Eve is no longer his definition of perfect. If Eve is reading romance novels, then Adam is no longer her definition of perfect. But in the first bedroom, there were no ghosts. There was perfection and comfort.

Whatever you think is the fundamental source of pleasure in life will become your god. In our culture, that's often sex; however, others view sex as dirty, as only a biological necessity but evil. The Bible takes the best parts of those views and gets rid of the worst parts. It says sex is biological but is also a great source of pleasure. In sex, you have the celebration of the like opposite nature of man and woman. You have a coming together, literally, that points to something nonliteral. In sex, the image of God is present because you have a very close representation of how two people can work together to accomplish one goal in the same way that the triune God does. Sex is fundamentally worship because sex images one God in three persons. Why does the Bible say that some sexual things are wrong? Because they fall outside the bounds of this idea of like otherness, of embracing the other.

The Bible's controversial views on sex and marriage are bound up in the doctrine of the Trinity. Some people view the biblical view of sexuality as an unimportant part of Christianity, but it is essential because the Trinity is essential. If you deny the Trinity, then you are not a

Christian. Sexuality is bound up in the Trinity. Why does the Bible say homosexuality is wrong? Homosexuality is not embracing the other. It is not "like oppositeness." It is "like likeness," and this loses the image of God. Sex is about a triune God saying something like "I have made like opposite people and they image me when they embrace the other. When they embrace the same, they do not image me." This is why in Romans 1, when Paul talks about homosexuality, he links it primarily to idolatry. Humans are saying, "I do not image God. I image me. I am not made to fulfill the purpose of God. I am made to fulfill the purpose of me." This is also why fornication is wrong. Why can't I have sex with whoever I want to have sex with? Why do we have to be married? Because marriage is the canvas on which the paint of gender is meant to shine. Because God made the marriage bed to be undefiled, in the words of Hebrews (13:4). God desired that there would not be any ghosts in the room. When God commands us to not have sex outside of marriage, he is saying it will cheapen and weaken your experience. It will bring ghosts into the bedroom; it will bring shame and guilt. God is for human flourishing. The God of the Bible is for great sex—but only as he defines great sex.

Fundamentally, to become a Christian is to say to God, "Not my ways, God, but your ways." If we think we can be Christians and think the Bible's wrong on sex, we are wrong, because we cannot say to God, "God, not my way but your way, unless we're talking about sex."

Our culture says that gender, marriage, and sex are about power and pleasure. The Bible says they are about purpose. They are for the purpose of serving God first and then serving other people. Gender is about serving the other in order to image God. God is primary; the other gender is secondary. Marriage is about serving your spouse, not yourself. In this, God's image is seen and your spouse is honored, appreciated, and loved. Sex is not primarily about you. It is about honoring and serving God and about honoring and serving your spouse.

Think of this like a hundred-piece puzzle. I dump out the box, then I pick up a piece. That piece exists to display the glory of the image of the whole puzzle. Have you ever put a puzzle together and one piece is missing? It cheapens the image of the whole. Your eyes automatically go to where the puzzle piece is missing. Each puzzle piece exists to glorify the whole, but it also exists to serve the other pieces, because if you are missing one piece, then the other pieces fail to reach their full potential. Each puzzle piece finds value and worth not in being a puzzle piece but in serving the whole and serving the pieces around it. Similarly, we find our meaning in gender, marriage, and sex by serving the whole. The full display is living out the image of the glory of God through serving those around us, our spouses, and others.

Ultimately, the purpose of gender, marriage, and sex is to point to Jesus. If these are about service, then who is the greatest servant of all time? Jesus. In marriage, the husband images Jesus by being the head of the home, the one who is answerable. Just as Jesus is the head of the church, the husband is the head of the home (Ephesians 5:23). The wife submits to the husband and is his helper (Ephesians 5:24). This status was not offensive for Jesus, who humbled himself and became a servant, even going to the cross (Philippians 2). If the husband says, "I do not want to be a leader; the leader job sucks," that is like saying, "Jesus, your job is worthless." When the wife says, "I do not want to be a helper. That job is worthless," that is like saying, "Jesus, your job is worthless." Jesus gives value to both the head and the servant. In marriage, both the husband and the wife uniquely image Jesus. The marriage of just the husband would be an authoritarian Jesus, and the marriage of just the wife would be an overly submissive Jesus. When they come together, they both display Jesus.

Marriage, sex, and gender point us to Jesus, who became a servant and embraced the other. Who was the other? We were the other. When he is on the cross and says, "My God, my God, why have you forsaken me?" (Matthew 27:46b) the answer is because Jesus has embraced sinners. Jesus became like a sinner in order to love and serve. On the cross, when he is suffering for our sin and transferring his righteousness to all who will believe, he is imaging perfectly what gender, marriage, and sex point to imperfectly.

The point of sex, marriage, and gender is to bring us to the one who embraced the other in an ultimate way. When you are around a great marriage, be reminded that it was designed by a God who came to Earth and loved you and served you perfectly. Your primary role, whether man or woman, single or married, wherever you are in life, is to image the glory of Jesus Christ and the gospel.

Chapter 4

Free or Fallen

Genesis 3

We've seen in Chapters 1 and 2 how God created the world to be a place of human flourishing, a place uniquely designed for humans to thrive and experience love and joy and peace. All of this is for the garden first and is then meant to spread around the world. If we were to stop there, we could say, "Based on those two chapters, this is a beautiful world." But it's not our world.

The question we have to wrestle with is this: "What happened to get us from that world to this world?" You don't have to hold to the biblical worldview to ask the question "What happened?" Every worldview, every religion, every culture throughout human history has asked the question "What went wrong?" In fact, sociologists point to it as one of the four or five basic worldview questions. You know all human cultures have asked this question because experientially, you have wondered this yourself. We have all come up against the tension of living in a world that is not whole and not healthy.

Sometimes, the unhealthiness of our world is very subtle. Your week can go well and you can say to yourself, "Life is good. The world is good," but experientially, you know that even when life is good, we are only pre-suffering. Sometimes you have to gain some age to understand this. Sadly, others suffer tragedy very early because of life experience. Some of us are pre-suffering, some of us are mid-suffering, while others are post-suffering. But even if you are post-suffering, this cycle just continues. When a tragedy strikes, when a natural disaster hits or there's a terrorist attack or an accident, it wakes us up from the dream that the world is healthy and right and good. No one sings "Zip-a-dee-do-da" at the cancer ward. We know our world is broken, but how did it get to be this way?

In Genesis, Moses is not primarily concerned with explaining physical things; he's concerned with explaining metaphysical things. That's why it only takes two chapters before he's answering the question "What went wrong?" Understanding Genesis 3 is foundational to understanding the Christian faith. If you understand Genesis 3, then the rest of Christianity makes sense. The chapter can be seen in three terms. First is cause: What's the cause of our world's condition? Second is consequences: What are the consequences of that cause? And finally, the cure: What cures our world's condition?

What Was the Cause?

Let's look at the cause of the world's condition. The easy biblical answer is to say the world is broken because of sin. But what is sin? Sin begins with a lie. The serpent comes up to Eve and says, "Did God actually say, 'You shall not eat of any tree in the garden'?" (Genesis 3:1). The serpent depicted here has been widely understood throughout Christian history to be Satan. When we think of Satan today, we typically think of a pitchfork and a tail and horns. We think of a guy in hell, torturing people. Or we may think of the Boogie Man. He is the great omniscient evil and he's conveniently around whenever we mess up so that we can say, "The devil made me do it." But these are not the Bible's depictions of Satan. The Bible depicts a person who does not run hell; rather, hell runs him. He is an enemy of God, but he's not everywhere and he's not the cause of all evil. But when he shows up, he whispers lies.

If you say, "There's great evil in the world!" you have one of two choices. Either you can say, "There is a spiritual reality" and that spiritual reality at least in some way answers why there is evil, or you can say, "There is no spiritual reality. Life is nothing but the physical." If you say, "There is a spiritual reality and that must have something to do with evil," the Bible agrees with you; it says this evil comes through Satan the whisperer. Genesis, and the Bible as a whole, is not a book of *Where's Satan?* It is not like the famous kids' book *Where's Waldo?* Satan is not wearing stripes and we are not supposed to be looking for him, but he is here in Genesis 3 and he is whispering. He's whispering, "Did God actually say, 'You shall not eat of any tree in the garden'?" (Genesis 3:1). Satan is whispering the lie of irreligion. He's essentially saying to Eve, "You can't trust God. Look at this instead." But notice what he does. God had told Adam and Eve, "You may surely eat of every tree of the garden, but of the tree of the knowledge of good and evil you shall not eat" (Genesis 2:16b–17a). Here comes Satan. If you read the Hebrew, it kind of reads like this: "Wow. God actually said you can't eat of any of these trees? Why would he say that?" But God didn't say anything like that. Satan knows very little about what God actually said. Instead, he's created an argument against God propped up by his own mythology. He comes to Eve and he's created a half-truth, a myth.

In fact, this thinking is true of so many people who have rejected Christianity. Only an honest wrestling with the message of Christianity will produce any results in your life. If you show up with half-truths and your own mythology, if you believe that you know the Bible but you've not read the Bible, or if you believe that you know about Jesus but you've not read the Gospels, then you don't know. So the first lie we believe is that we don't need to listen to God. We can form our own conclusions about God and then decide we don't need

God. That is what's going on here; it is a lie of irreligion. God tells Adam to eat from any tree, just not this one tree. And Satan shows up and implies, "Wow! What kind of God puts you in a garden and says, 'Don't eat of any trees'?"

But there's another lie as well. In Genesis 3:2–3, we read, "And the woman said to the serpent, 'We may eat of the fruit of the trees in the garden, but God said, "You shall not eat of the fruit of the tree that is in the midst of the garden, neither shall you touch it, lest you die."'" Did God really say, "If you touch the tree, you will die"? No, he did not. In fact, Eve hadn't even been created when God said anything about the tree. Eve wasn't even there, but she has told herself she can't even touch it. But that's not true. She could have built a tree house in it. Eve could have pulled the fruit off and made a centerpiece for the table. She could have squeezed the juice and used it as paint. God didn't say, "Don't touch it; don't sleep under it; don't climb it; don't build a tree house." He simply said, "You shall not eat … of it" (Genesis 2:17b).

What you have here is the lie of irreligion from Satan and the lie of religion from Eve. Satan comes up and undermines God by implying, "Oh, God, you can't trust him. He's no good. Even if there was a god, what kind of a god would put you in a garden and tell you not to eat fruit off any of the trees? Do you even want that kind of god? Do you see the dilemma I've created?" And Eve replies with the following logic from her own mind: "There is a god, and we're not supposed to eat from this tree or touch it." Eve has built an extra set of rules around the rule that God created. This is the lie of religion. You've got Satan making up things, and you've got Eve making up things. The woman does what most religious people do: She builds rules around God's rules and says, basically, "My relationship with God is about performance. I can stay in the garden as long as I don't touch, as long as I don't eat, and as long as I don't do. My staying here is about my own performance," rather than saying what is true: The tree is an evidence that she is not God. It's a boundary.

Satan's lie does what all lies do: It changes our view of reality. This is why lies are dangerous: They change the way we see the world. The serpent seizes on the lie Eve believes. He says, "You will not surely die, for God knows that when you eat of it, your eyes will be opened and you will be like God, knowing good and evil" (Genesis 3:4b–5). Here's Satan's second lie: "Is it a good thing or bad thing to know evil? It's bad!"

Eve already knew good. When God was creating the world, what does Moses say over and over again? "And God saw that it was good" (Genesis 1:4, 10, 18, 21, 25, 31). Eve knows good, and the serpent tells her that God wants to keep the knowledge of good and evil from her. Well, that's a good thing to keep from somebody! When the lie of irreligion convinces us that God is not good, it changes the way we view God. It changes our view of reality so that when we see God, when we see the things that he does, and when we read the Scriptures, we go, "Eh." That is what's happening here.

Look at what happens to the woman. She's very religious; she's built the extra rule—don't even touch the tree. Then Moses writes, "So when the woman saw that the tree was good for food, and that it was a delight to the eyes … " (Genesis 3:6a). She's already beginning to doubt the rules she's created, so all of a sudden, what was bad now becomes good. Jealousy is a great example of this. When you begin to believe the lie that you can't trust your spouse or partner, it will poison your relationship, because when you believe a lie, it changes your view of reality. The serpent is giving a lie, and Eve is believing a lie and it's poisoning Eve's view of reality. All of a sudden, a tree that she walked past a million times and said, "I don't care about that, I've got all these other trees, and I've got Adam, and we've got this job to subdue and fill the earth," has caught her attention and now she sees nothing but the tree.

That brings us to the third thing that's true of sin. Sin begins with a lie, then it changes our view of reality, and finally, it replaces God with something else. Look at the end of verse 6: "So when the woman saw that the tree was good for food, and that it was a delight to the eyes, and that the tree was to be desired to make one wise … "When Eve becomes convinced that God is not out for her good, that the only way she can relate to God is on the basis of performance, it changes her view of reality. She replaces God with this idea of being wise. Eve is not just believing a lie, the lie has changed her view. She no longer wants God; she wants so-called wisdom. She doesn't want God; she wants to be God.

No lie is neutral, and every lie provides something in its place. Every lie you believe says, "Not that, this," and Eve's lie says, "Not God, being wise like God." If you're skeptical of God, all your lie has done is provide you a different kind of faith—faith in the fact that the idea of God is stupid. You're building your life on a faith claim, just like you would have been had you believed in God, but the lie has given you something else in God's place. If you say, "God only cares about performance. He relates to us on the basis of dos and don'ts. Don't touch. Don't think. Don't say. Don't do this. Do that," then this lie has given you rules to follow instead of God. Every lie provides something else in God's place. The human condition, not just of Adam and Eve, but also of all of us post-Adam and Eve, is that we have believed a lie. The lie has changed our view of reality, and it has replaced God with other things.

What Are the Consequences?

What are the consequences of believing this lie that God is not good, that he's not out to help us, that he is actually out to restrict us and deprive us? The lie affects every single thing about Adam and Eve.

First, there's a spiritual consequence. In believing that God is not good and in seeing that the tree all of a sudden is good because the tree provides what God will not provide, Adam and Eve replace God with the tree. The tree offers to them the knowledge of evil. Because they believe the lie, they now want evil, so they pursue it and the world crumbles. Look what happens in Genesis 3:8: "And they heard the sound of the LORD God walking in the garden in the cool of the day, and the man and wife hid themselves from the presence of the LORD."You can't understand that verse unless you've read Genesis 1 and 2, where everything is described as good. God speaks to man, man speaks to God, God speaks to woman, and it's good and right and pure, and they're naked and there's no shame or guilt. Now when God shows up, the people that he created, the people that he put in a land for human flourishing, are running from him.

What we have here is a disconnect between God and humanity. Why? Because humanity has believed a lie that God is not good. You may say, "I don't believe the lie that God is not good," but we all do. We do it irreligiously by saying, "I don't need that spirituality stuff." Or we do it religiously by saying, "God is not good; he's out to get me, but if I keep these rules, I can stop God from getting me." It doesn't matter which way the lie manifests itself. It poisons our relationship with God because we have believed a lie that God is not good.

The Bible says we are all born into that lie. The best metaphor I can think of for this is a country in the midst of a civil war, and a rebellious group springs up and says, "This is not our government anymore; we want our own way." If your parents belong to that rebellion and you're born into that rebellion, you become a rebel by default. You're born a rebel, you're raised a rebel, and you join the rebellion. And that is what the Bible says about humanity: We believed the lie. We rebelled against God, and we are born into the rebellion.

The impact is not just spiritual; it's psychological. Look at verse 7: "Then the eyes of both were opened." They now know both good and evil, and they know that they are naked. Their eyes are open, and each worries what the other is thinking, so they cover themselves up. There's shame and guilt, regret and insecurity. You have the man saying, "The woman whom you gave to be with me, she gave me fruit" (Genesis 3:12a). You have a man who's not only broken but also a blame-shifter. He can't even own up to it. The Bible says when we believed the lie that God is not good, it plunged us into a psychological situation in which we are destined to live out a cycle of guilt, shame, and disappointment. This is instantly what happens. Adam and Eve are plunged into insecurity, guilt, condemnation, and regret. This cycle will repeat throughout the book of Genesis, throughout the Bible, and throughout our own lives.

The Bible says human beings are psychologically broken. We're born into the world wanting to fill a hole. We don't know why the hole is there and we don't know what to use to fill it. We try to fill it with all different kinds of things. We put career, family, sex, relationship, and money into this hole, and we just keep trading them out, saying, "Life is about this and life is about that." But they never really provide us with what we're looking for, because what we're looking for is what only God can provide, so we're plunged into psychological broken-ness. We're plunged into guilt, shame, and regret. Many people in the irreligious crowd will say that it's actually religion that produces guilt, shame, and regret, and if we could just get rid of religion, people wouldn't feel guilty all the time. However, the God of the Bible creates a world with no guilt or shame until we want guilt and shame.

What is the lie we believe? "You don't know evil, and you should know evil. God is keeping something from you." And the minute we took the fruit, our first parents took the fruit and bit it, evil came rushing into our world. That's why it's there. And yes, that came with guilt, shame, and regret. So when someone says, "If it wasn't for Christianity there wouldn't be guilt," that's false. The first two chapters of Genesis are the world as Christianity desires it to be and there's no guilt or shame.

Sin also affects us relationally. Eve takes the fruit and she eats, and not only does she eat, but she gives some to Adam. There were only two people in the garden, so when they get naked and feel ashamed, from who are they feeling shame? Eventually, God shows up and they hide from God, but he's not there right now. They're covering up from each other. Already, we have a brokenness of intimacy. We are relationally broken and we are also broken in terms of how we relate to each other within marriage. Look at verse 16: "To the woman he said, 'I will surely multiply your pain in childbearing; in pain you shall bring forth children. Your desire shall be for your husband and he shall rule over you.'" God is saying there's going to be marital conflict: She's going to want things that she can't have, and he's going to want things that he can't have. Brokenness manifests itself relationally in one of two ways. Either we blame each other when things go bad or we want things from each other that we can't provide.

Sin affects us spiritually, psychologically, relationally, and, finally, naturally. God says the earth itself is now broken because of what Adam and Eve have done (Genesis 3:17–19). You have God, then you have humanity, and then you have Earth. When humanity gets out of whack, nature gets out of whack. God tells Adam that when he works the ground, it's going to be difficult; he's going to have to harvest. The natural universe is broken. With all of this brokenness, you finally see that this is what God meant when he said to Adam they would die if they ate from the tree.

But they don't die; they don't drop dead immediately. But God doesn't mean only physical death. He means a holistic, spiritual, psychological, emotional, natural death. He means, "Your relationship with each other is going to die. Your relationship with yourself and your psychological makeup are going to die. You're going to die spiritually." And that's exactly what happens.

If you look into our culture for answers to the existence of evil, if you grab someone out of the culture and say, "Why does evil exist?" they'll give you one of several answers. They will say, "Evil exists because of our psychology," or "Evil exists because of our sociology, our relationships," or "Evil exists because we're broken chemically," or "It's bad parenting," or "Evil exists because it's natural. Survival of the fittest. That implies evil. We have to hurt each other to get there." Or they will say, "It's spiritual." Only the Bible says it's all of those things. Only the Bible says those things are not the cause, they're the consequences. So if you said to the Bible, "There's evil because of broken psychology," the Bible would agree, but then it would say something like

"There's broken psychology because humanity has believed a lie." If you said to the Bible, "There's evil because of bad parenting, bad social structures, bad school systems, and bad criminal justice systems," the Bible would say these exist because of a lie. Maybe you say, "Evil is natural." The Bible's story of Adam and Eve informs us that evil didn't used to be natural but now it is. Only the Bible has this holistic understanding of the evil in our universe.

What Is the Cure?

If we're going to cure this evil, we've got to go back to the cause. We can't start with consequences. We can get to the consequences, but we can't start there. We've got to deal with the lie. The irreligious person says, "That's the problem with the world; the whole concept of God is causing our world to disintegrate." The religious person says, "God is out to get me, but if I keep the rules, he can't get me." But either way, it's the same lie: God is not good, and he's out to get me.

But move forward in Genesis 3 and you will read, "And the LORD God made for Adam and for his wife garments of skins and clothed them" (Genesis 3:21). Immediately, God shows Adam and Eve that he does not desire their harm but desires their good. One of the first acts of God, post Adam and Eve eating the fruit, is to cover them, to create something for them. There's grace there. There is love there and God is implying through his actions, "I haven't stopped loving you. I haven't stopped caring about you. You're still made in my image." God instantly reacts to the lie and shows Adam and Eve that he is out for their good by making them loincloths. When God makes the animal skins for them, it comes at a cost. God has to interject himself and he has to kill a couple of animals.

God points to something greater he's going to do that's going to come at a greater cost. He says to the serpent, "I will put enmity between you and the woman, and between your offspring and her offspring; he shall bruise your head, and you shall bruise his heel" (Genesis 3:15). He's essentially saying to the serpent, "There will be someone that I'm going to send, and when that someone gets here, he is going to crush what you've done, and it's going to come at a cost. He's going to be hurt. But he will overcome you, just as here I'm overcoming what you've done. Now it's just a few animals to make animal skins, but there's a day coming when it will be greater than that." Who is this guy? Who did it? The answer is Jesus.

When does Jesus face down the serpent and crush his head? It does not begin on the cross. It begins at Jesus's temptation in the wilderness. Jesus goes into the wilderness, and Satan says the same kinds of lies he said to Adam and Eve. Satan twists the words of God and he even quotes scripture, but Jesus's answer every time can be summed up with the words "I trust the goodness of God." In his temptation, Jesus does what Adam and Eve could not do: He defeats Satan by trusting in the goodness of God, therefore not believing the lies of Satan—the lies of irreligion or religion (Matthew 4:1–11).

Not only does God deal with the cause, but he also deals with the consequences. After Adam and Eve eat from the tree, God says, "'Behold, the man has become like one of us in knowing good and evil. Now, lest he reach out his hand and take also of the tree of life and eat and live forever—' therefore the LORD God sent him out from the garden of Eden to work the ground from which he was taken. He drove out the man and at the east of the garden of Eden he placed the cherubim and a flaming sword that turned every way to guard the way to the tree of life" (Genesis 3:22b–24). God knows Adam and Eve are spiritually, psychologically, relationally, and naturally dead and if they live forever in this way, that will be an awful existence.

The immediate way that God deals with the consequences is by driving Adam and Eve out from the garden so the consequences will not be eternally permanent. The final way Jesus defeats Satan is by going to the cross. Jesus never believes the lies of Satan; he always believes the goodness of God. He never has his view of reality changed. He never replaces God with anything else. He only ever does what God does. As he marches to the cross and as he gets on the cross, what does he experience? He experiences spiritual alienation. What does he say on the cross but "My God, my God, why have you forsaken me?" (Matthew 27:46)? Here, he also experiences psychological disconnect. He experiences the ultimate relational detachment when he's on the cross and the spectators are yelling, "Crucify him! Crucify him!" (Luke 23:21). Finally, the Bible says when Jesus was crucified, when he was ultimately murdered, nature went nuts; there were even natural disasters (Matthew 27:51).

On the cross, Jesus comes as the one God promised in Genesis 3, the one who never listenes to the lie, the one who always believes God, but he goes to the cross and suffers the consequences of our choice in order that God might rescue us. On the cross, Jesus, who does not deserve any of these consequences, subjects himself to them in order that God might take our sin and put it on Jesus, and then take Jesus's righteousness and put it on us. What does it mean to be a Christian? To be a Christian is to say that not only did Adam and Eve make a mess of the world but that I also participate in the mess; I was born to rebel parents; I am a rebel; I participate in the rebellion against God; therefore, I need grace. God has shown me grace in the person of Jesus Christ, so my faith is in Jesus, who took my consequences so I could be free from them and turn from my former rebellion in order to serve God. That's, in essence, what it means to be a Christian.

If you ask the Bible, "Why is there evil in the world?" the answer will be because we believe a lie—not just because Adam and Eve believed a lie but because we still believe the lie. The Bible says that God became a man and endured all our brokenness in order to die in our place to make atonement. He took the penalty of God for our sin, crushed the enemy, and then raised from the dead, inviting us to turn from rebellion and to turn toward grace. To say, "The problem with the world is sin" is incredibly simplistic. There is real psychological brokenness. There is real relational brokenness. There's sexual brokenness. There's spiritual brokenness. But the remedy for these things first must aim at the cause, not the consequences. And the only real remedy for the cause is the gospel of Jesus Christ.

Chapter 5

Goodness or Grace?

Genesis 4:1–16

It is easy to see we have a great world in the beginning of Genesis. We have a world that was designed for our flourishing. Because Adam and Eve eat from a particular tree, our world is broken, so I am broken and the world is broken because of them. It does not seem fair. Why would we be made to pay for their sin? Why would I suffer the consequences?

As we ask these questions, we get to the story of Cain and Abel. We have the story of two brothers, and one brother murders the other. Why is this included immediately after the garden? It is to show us that it is not just the sin of Adam and Eve that we passively come up under. Cain is meant to be a mirror into our own souls. This makes us recoil because Cain is, in fact, a murderer.

One of the biggest components of the human rebellion against God is that we actually think we are better than we really are. The most important verse in all of Genesis 4 is verse 7. In verse 7, we see a simple warning from God to Cain. This warning is pre-murder. "And God says to Cain, 'Sin is crouching at your door. It's desire is for you, but you must rule over it'" (Genesis 4:7). You are going to see that everything in Genesis 4 is understood in light of this verse—everything that comes before it and everything that comes after it.

First, we must see, through Cain, that we all overestimate our goodness. Second, we also see that we underestimate the power of our sin—which raises a question: How can we acknowledge both of these things without being crushed?

Overestimated Goodness

God tells Cain in verse 7 that sin is crouching at the door. God is warning Cain that he is on the precipice of disaster. He is saying, "Cain, I want you to know that you are standing at the top of a slippery slope. Sin is crouching." The crouching metaphor there implies that there is a pouncing coming. It is passive now but it is going to be attacking soon. It is going to destroy him.

On the surface, Cain seems to be a really good guy. In the beginning of Genesis 4, Eve has Cain, her firstborn, and says, "The Lord has blessed me with a man" (Genesis 4:1b). Cain is born into a home where they understand the relationship of God's grace to their very existence. Adam and Eve were in the garden. They know what they have done. They know they have been kicked out of the garden. They know they deserve not just spiritual, emotional, and psychological death but also natural death. They know that their very existence and ability to have children is through the grace of God.

The very first thing we see Cain do is bring an offering to the Lord (Genesis 4:3). The Hebrew word used here for offering shows it is not just any kind of offering Cain is making. He is making what is called a dedication offering. The whole point of bringing the offering is to say, "All that I have, I have only because of the grace of God." On the surface, Cain looks very good, but there is a problem here. Abel and

Cain come to make an offering, and the Bible says that God "had regard for Abel and his offering, but for Cain and his offering he had no regard" (Genesis 4:4b–5a). God's primary concern here is not with the offering, it is with the offerer. Why does God prefer one offering to the next? Is it because Abel offers animals and a blood sacrifice and Cain offered vegetables? Is it because Abel offers the fatty portions and Cain offers just regular garden-variety vegetables? Moses tells us that God does not accept Abel's offering first but accepts Abel first and *then* his offering (Genesis 4:4). God does not accept Cain and then does not accept his offering (Genesis 4:5). Why? In Hebrews 11, we are told that God accepts Abel's sacrifice because it is offered in faith.

What does that mean? When Abel shows up saying, "God, everything I have is because of you, so take this offering," he actually means it. Abel really does believe, in going through his day, that if it was not for the grace of God shown to his parents, if it was not for the goodness of God being shown to him every day, he would not be who he is and doing what he is doing, but Cain shows up and has no faith. He is going through the religious motions, but he does not actually believe in what he is doing. The result of this, we are told, is that God has no regard for him. This means that God blesses Abel's life and does not bless Cain's. Cain recognizes that his not being blessed by God is ultimately connected to the fact that he has halfheartedly worshipped God.

Cain is very angry, and his face falls (Genesis 4:5b). He is saying, "Wait a minute. I get up every morning. I work hard. I am religious. I am raised in a religious home. I go and I do the worship. I do the offering thing. And you bless Abel and you do not bless me? That is not fair. I am angry. You do not give me what it is that I need, but you give it to Abel," yet when God shows up to deal with Cain, God shows up not to judge Cain but to counsel him.

God shows up, but he is not angry with Cain. Instead, he is warning Cain. He says, "Cain, why are you angry? Are you right to be angry? Do you not know that if you do good, I will accept you. If you do not do good, I am not going to accept you" (Genesis 4:6). Then he says, in verse 7, "Sin is crouching at the door." God is counseling Cain. The Christian God, the God of the Bible, when he finds people mired in sin, when he finds them angry, when he finds them in doubt, when he finds them frustrated, shows up first not as a judge but as a counselor, and he says, "Do not do this. Your sin is crouching."

By crouching, God has in mind a crouching predator. He is saying to Cain, "You think your problem is insignificant. You think you are harboring this bitterness in the corner of your heart, but I am telling you, sin is just crouching. That is why it looks small to you. It is crouching, but it is going to pounce." God is saying to Cain, "Your problem is much larger than you think." We can think of this another way: God is saying to Cain that his sin is like an iceberg. He is saying to Cain, "You are looking out over the water of your life and you see a little bit of ice sticking out over the water. You are leaving it there. You are letting it just float out on the water, but underneath the tip of that is this massive mountain of bitterness, anger, frustration, self-righteousness, and halfheartedness. If you leave these things there, sin will eventually destroy your ship, your life. If you let the predator crouch, if you let it lull you into complacency, it is going to pounce and it is going to destroy you."

What is going on in Cain? Why does a person show up to worship halfheartedly? If your heart is not into it, why not just stay home? If he does not believe it, why does he not just sit out on it? Because he does not show up to give anything to God. He shows up to get something from God.

Cain is punching the clock. He is showing up to church, putting his card in, andsaying, "God, I did what I did; now you give me what you are supposed to give me." He is not only an idolater; he is a self-idolater. Cain believes that if he does what he is supposed to do, God then must do what he is supposed to do. In essence, Cain is saying, "God is a puppet and I am the puppeteer. And as long as I move my hands the right way, as long as I hit the right buttons, as long as I go through the motions, and as long as I do my religious duty, God must bless me." That's what is going on in halfhearted worship.

Do you see the difference between Cain and Abel? This is so significant because what we do and what Cain is doing is making light of his sin. God says that when we gather, we all talk about the tip of our icebergs but we are ignorant that there is something underneath them. God says, "Your heart is in the worship of you. Your heart is not in the demands from me."

My seminary president used to say, "If you would cheat on your test, you would cheat on your wife." This means every act of deception has a mountain of lies underneath it. Do you know when the little tip of something is an iceberg? When the water level drops. When you allow the mountain of deception to stay in your life, all it takes is a change in the water level for you to be absolutely destroyed. That is what God is saying to Cain. God says that sin is crouching. What he means is that sin, by its very nature, makes itself strategically small. That is why we all keep pet sins in our lives. But God says, "No. There are no little pieces of ice; they are all icebergs. There are no crouching predators that are not dangerous. All of these things will absolutely destroy and ruin you."

What are the things floating on the surface of your life that you know about? Where is your weakness? What God is saying to you is "Do not ignore that weakness. There is a mountain underneath it." We know the story of Cain and Abel as a story of murder, but this is the 30,000-foot view. We can look at Cain's life and say, "Cain! Listen to him! You are three sentences away from murder!" but we do not have that perspective in ourlives. We have the two-foot view of our own lives. We see what is in front of us, but what God says to us is the same thing he says to Cain: "You are three sentences away from ruining your life." Your only hope is that you acknowledge that it is not a little thing floating on top of the water but is a massive thing that can absolutely destroy you."

Why do we overestimate our goodness? We say things like "I am a good person except for ____. I am not like those psychos out there." If you study history, you find that the people who do the most evil were not psychos at all. They were ordinary people who held on to mountains of sin and the water level changed. God is saying, "Your relationships, psychology, and emotions are three sentences away from being broken. When the water level changes, you do not change; the real you is simply exposed."

Underestimated Sin

Not only do we overestimate our goodness, we underestimate the power of sin. Why does an animal crouch? It crouches to pounce. When God says to Cain, "Sin is crouching at your door," the implication is that it is going to pounce. God says right after that, "Its desire is for you." God is coming to Cain as a counselor, not yet as a judge.

We know the story of Cain and Abel as a story of murder. Cain shows up to worship halfheartedly. He does not really believe in his offering; he is just going through the motions. He is not saying to God, "Thank you, God, for what I get from you," but instead, "God, here. Take this. Now give me." That is how he shows up to worship. You have no idea what is going on in his soul. Getting bitter with God never satisfies you, because God is not there to yell at. Cain, instead of directing his anger and bitterness at God, shifts and directs it at his brother. He says, "God does not like me because he compares me to my brother. But if my brother did not exist, God would have to accept me." Cain becomes bitter with his brother.

Can we not identify with every one of those steps? Are you honest? Are you introspective enough to say, "Yes, I can understand getting frustrated with God because I have done my duty but he has not blessed me." Then you are Cain. The difference between Cain and us is not that Cain is a murderer and we would never murder. The difference is that our sin is still in crouch mode. Cain's has already unleashed its fury. When we look at our lives from the two-foot view, we never believe this, yet God tells us every lust is adultery waiting to happen. Every anger is murder waiting to happen. Bitterness is poison to your own soul waiting to happen. Power is greed waiting to happen.

In the famous Sermon on the Mount, what does Jesus say about crouching sin? "You have heard that it was said, 'You shall not commit adultery.' But I say to you that everyone who looks at a woman with lustful intent has already committed adultery with her in his heart" (Matthew 5:27–28). He is saying the only difference between you and the adulterer is that your water level has not dropped. For some of you, the only thing standing between you and murder, between you and adultery, between you and standing over people, is that you are a coward. You are not good. I am not good. We are cowards.

The Bible says we overestimate our goodness. We suppress. We overestimate our goodness and underestimate the power of sin. It happened to Cain. Do you think Cain thinks, *In six sentences, I am going to murder my brother*? No, but halfhearted worship, which is really self-idolatry, ultimately leads not just to murder but also to premeditated murder.

Some of us know we have been mastered by sin. You may not want to look at pornography anymore, but you do. You do not want to be bitter anymore, but you are. You are living what Cain lived. You are experiencing what God told him he would experience.

Now What?

How can we acknowledge these two realities without being crushed? First, we are far worse than we ever imagine. Second, the evil that is in us will absolutely wreck us. Genesis 4 is telling us we are worse than we ever dared to imagine. How can we believe that and not come away crushed?

There are two ways that we are prone to dealing with this. First, you can try the irreligious way. You can ignore it and think, *I am good. It is just a piece of ice. It is just a crouching lion in the corner of the room. I am okay.* Cain did that. You can ignore it, but it will wreck you. The other approach is to be religious. You can look inwardly and say, "If I have overestimated my goodness and I have underestimated the power of sin, then I must amp up my goodness. The only answer is to be honest with myself. I haven't been good enough. Okay. I am going to be better. I am going to try harder. I am going to do more." The problem with both these views is that sin is greater than we can ever imagine. Even when we think we have beaten it, we have not. But if we succeed and we become even better than we are now, where will we look for gratitude? We will look inwardly and be exactly what Cain was: a self-idolater. Looking inward or ignoring it is not the answer, so what do we do?

When God shows up in Genesis 4, he always shows up in grace. First, we see Cain and Abel bringing him offerings. Why are they doing this? Because in the garden, God did not destroy Adam and Eve. No Adam and Eve means no Cain and Abel. This grace points back to Genesis 3:15, where God says, "I'll fix this." Abel shows up with his offering, saying, "My only hope is that you will fix this." Cain shows up saying, "My only hope is that you will give me what I want." But God is there in grace. Then, when Cain goes through the motions, when God does not bless him, when Cain gets angry, God shows up and warns him. Cain ignores God. Then, the third time God shows up, he judges Cain. He says, "You have murdered your brother; you have got to get out of here. You are not going to be able to work the ground anymore. Life is going to be difficult for you. I have to punish you. I am a just God. Abel was innocent and you murdered him in cold blood; you must be punished." Cain responds in anger: "Here you go being unfair again. You have destroyed me. I have no hope." God says, "No, I'll put a mark on you so no one will harm you." This is God's grace on Cain. He is saying, "Even though you have done this, I'll protect you from others" (Genesis 4:11–15).

Everywhere God shows up He shows up in grace. This is important because the beginning point of acknowledging that we are far worse than we ever imagined, that we are three sentences away from destruction and yet we are not crushed is to believe not only that there is a God but that he is a God of grace. If it is any other God, we have no hope. If he has anything for us beyond grace, we have no hope. If he is expecting us to clean up, we have no hope. If he is expecting us to fix it, we have no hope. The lie of religion or of irreligion tells us that if we turn to God in honesty, he will destroy us. Christianity tells us it is only by going to God and saying, "Here is who I really am," that any of us have any hope.

Look at where God shows up and says, "Where is Abel your brother?" (Genesis 4:9a). God is giving Cain a chance to repent. Cain replies, "I do not know; am I my brother's keeper?" (Genesis 4:9b). And God says, "Cain, do you not hear? Abel's blood is screaming at me from the ground. I am God, Cain. I know." He is waiting for Cain to say, "Oh, God, you are so right; I am so sick. I am so devastated," but Cain will not say it. The biggest danger, the biggest piece of that iceberg floating under the water, is our inability to be honest with ourselves and honest with God. Our only hope is that God is a god of grace, which means we can go to him and say, "God, I am far worse than I ever thought. I have no hope of fixing myself."

How is he going to fix us? How is he going to make it better? Look at verse 10. When Cain will not repent, where does God take him? God takes him to blood and says, "What have you done? The voice of your brother's blood is crying out to me from the ground." God is saying, "Look, Cain. Here is evidence of what you have done." He is demanding repentance. Abel, the wholehearted worshiper, was killed by Cain, the halfhearted worshiper, because Abel's very existence indicted Cain. Every time Abel went to worship and he meant it, and every time God blessed him as a result, it was just one more dagger in Cain's side. Cain could not take it, to the point that he murdered Abel. Abel's blood cried for justice.

Abel points us to a greater Abel. Abel is not the only wholehearted worshiper to be murdered by halfhearted worshipers because his existence indicted them. Jesus Christ, when he was on Earth, lived as a wholehearted worshiper. He would say things like "Whatever I see the Father doing, that's what I do" (John 5:19–20). Every time he was around the sick and the poor, he cared about them more than himself. He was never selfish, never greedy, never bitter, never filled with lust, and never filled with anger. He was a wholehearted worshiper. What do you think happened? Have you ever been around a person who's better than you? Does it produce in you joy over the fact that they are better than you? No, it produces bitterness and rage. And we are filled with that. We were not there when Cain murdered Abel, but we were there in spirit and are capable of doing the same thing. Eventually, Jesus is murdered by halfhearted worshipers who are saying, "If we had been just one more minute around you, it would have absolutely crushed us because you expose us for the liars we are." But while the first Abel's blood cries out for justice, the second Abel's blood cries out for forgiveness.

Hebrews 12 says that Jesus is the mediator of a new covenant and his sprinkled blood speaks a better word than the blood of Abel. The Bible is saying, "Listen, all of us are being pursued by God and God will ask us, 'What have you done?' and we will either cling to the blood of Abel or the blood of Jesus." When we deny and suppress our sin and say things like "I am a good person! I don't deserve this!" God will take us to the blood of Abel—not the Abel in this story, but all the Abels we have stepped on, all the Abels we have hurt, all the Abels we have ignored, and all the Abels we have mistreated. He will take us to that blood and say, "What am I to do? Their blood cries out for your judgment."

But for those of us who fling ourselves at the mercy of God's grace, for those of us who do what Cain should have done and said, "Oh God! I am so sick, I have murdered my own brother! Help me! Save me! Rescue me!"—for all of us who do that, there is a better blood. The blood of Jesus Christ. We have to go to God saying, "God, I am a halfhearted worshiper who participated in the murder of the greatest worshiper ever to live, Jesus Christ. My only hope is that he did not die by my hand first but by your hand. My only hope is that he came to Earth to mediate a better covenant. My only hope is that the blood he spilled was for my forgiveness. My only hope is that on the cross, Jesus dies for my rebellion. He died because I have sinned against you, and he did it willingly so my sin might be put on him and his righteousness on me. My only hope is that that satisfies your judgment so I can get your grace."

What does it mean to be a Christian? It does not mean to clean yourself up. It does not mean to wrestle the lion in the corner of the room. It does not mean to go grab a pick, swim under water, and start chipping away at the iceberg. It means to go to God and say, "I am sick. I am diseased. I am sinful. I'm three sentences away from being crushed, and my only hope is that you are a gracious God who has shed his blood for me on the cross so that I do not have to answer to the blood of Abel but the blood of Jesus."

Three times, God comes to Cain with grace. Three times, Cain rejects God. Do not become Cain. Do not be so hardened in your sin. Do not become so self-righteous, so self-focused, that even now as God says, "Turn to my grace and I will accept you. Turn to Jesus and I will accept you," you say, "No, I do not need it; I am good." Instead, be like Abel, who, in the beginning of the story, comes to God and says, "It is only by your goodness and your grace that I stand." Whose blood will speak for you, Abel's or Jesus's?

Chapter 6

Right or Righteous

Genesis 6:5–7:24

We come to the story of Noah and the ark. This is not a children's story. Rather, the emphasis in this story is on God himself. In Genesis 6:8, we see "Noah found favor in the eyes of the Lord," yet we do not hear from God at all. It is intentional that we do not hear from God. He is showing us what happens when humanity turns away from God and turns inward: God is not to be found. If you want to turn your back on God, God will let you. If you want to walk the other direction, God will let you. What does God see? What does God say? What is God's plan? And finally, how do we respond to God's plan? I want to take our attention off of ourselves, bring it back to God, and simply look at this passage with three questions: What does the flood tell us about God? What does the ark tell us about God? Finally, did the flood work?

What Does the Flood Tell Us about God?

We see from the flood that the God of the Bible is personally invested in this world. Genesis 6:5–6 says, "The Lord saw that the wickedness of man was great in the earth and that every intention of the thoughts of his heart was only evil continually. And the LORD regretted that he had made man on the earth and it grieved him to his heart." The God of the Bible is intimately aware of the state of the earth. He is aware of the oppressor and the oppressed. He is aware of the tyrant and those under tyranny. He knows everybody all the time. This is not what all worldviews and all world religions say about God. In fact, this is the opposite of the deistic view that God created the world like a clock-maker only to leave it ticking on its own. This is a God who is con-ceptual but not practical. The questions we must ask are these: Where is God? Does he care? Does he know what is happening? Truthfully, we all have asked that question. Does he care? The Bible overwhelm-ingly says, "Yes!"

The God of the Bible cares about this world. He knows what is going on in this world. Nothing catches him by surprise, and that is a good thing. It is a good thing that God is intimately and actively involved in our world, but it leads to a second point, which we might not find as exciting. God is not only personally involved in this world but also takes all sin personally. What is sin? Sin is believing a lie about God. It is taking the truth of God and saying, "No, not that. This." It is saying to God, "I am God, not you," or "This is God, not you." All sin is per-sonal to God. Look at Genesis 6:7: "So the Lord said, 'I will blot out man whom I have created from the face of the land, for I am sorry that I have made them.'" The word "sorry" here, which is the same Hebrew word that is used earlier for the word "regretted," can literally be translated "to console oneself." Verse 7 in this context can read, "So the Lord said, 'I will blot out man whom I have created from the face of the land, for I am consoling myself that I have made him.'" In other words, all sin wounds God personally. This is something that no other religion would say. Not only is God personally invested in this world, but he has decided to so join himself to this world that he takes all sin personally. Every occasion on which you have looked at God, shaken your fist at God, or maybe even shaken a particular finger at God and said, "God, it is not your way that is best; it is my way that is best," he takes personally. All sin is not just turning toward something that is wrong but turning away from God first and then turning toward something that is wrong.

Imagine if I were to commit adultery against my wife. What would hurt my wife more than anything would not be the sexual act I committed with another woman. It would be first that I rejected her. Most damaging in our marriage would be that I essentially said, "You cannot provide for me what I need; I find pleasure outside of you. I find comfort outside of you. I find joy outside of you." The Bible says the same is true of God. When we sin against God, we are fundamentally saying, "God, you are not great."

In Genesis 3, the fundamental problem with Eve is that she says to God, "You have lied to me. You have kept wisdom from me, and I can find true wisdom somewhere other than you." I can give a very fundamental example to show that you do this. Have you ever done something that your conscience has told you not to do? The Bible tells us that the conscience is a gift of common grace from God and is given to all people (Romans 2:12–16). In that moment when your conscience says, "This is not best. This is not right. This is not okay," that is the grace of God in your life saying, "Do not do this." And yet what do we do? We suppress it.

Genesis 6:11 says, "Now the Earth was corrupt in God's sight." We all want a God who is personally and actively involved in our world, do we not? The implication is that we want God to be there, but the reality is that if God is with us, if God is present, if God loves us so much, he is around. If he is in this room right now, then everything we do and everything we think and everything we say is in his sight.

If God sees into our innermost thoughts and hearts every minute of every day, none of us are good. You are not a good person just because you learn how to suppress your evil, you know how to bite your tongue, or you know how to keep everything in the back of your mind. If God knows what is in our hearts and minds, if he is so intimately involved in this world that he sees us at our very core, then we are all in trouble. This leads us to another thing we learn about God from the flood: God must judge us.

This can be a very unpopular concept, but let's unpack this for a minute. Look at the judgment language in Genesis 6:11–13: "Now the Earth was corrupt in God's sight and the Earth was filled with violence. And God saw the Earth and behold, it was corrupt, for all flesh had corrupted their way on the Earth. And God said to Noah, 'I am determined to make an end to all flesh for the Earth is filled with violence through them. Behold, I will destroy them with the Earth.'" Then Noah and his family get in the ark and the animals get in the ark. Genesis 7:16 says, "And the Lord shut them in." That is judgment language. Who closes the ark door? God does. What are we to do with God and his judgment? What are we to do with the story of the flood? How could we believe in and love a God like this?

God is telling us that turning away from him and turning toward ourselves has devastating consequences, and not just for us. There is a ripple effect when we turn away from God and we turn toward ourselves. When we turn away from God and we turn toward ourselves, we increase the number of victims on the Earth. We leave victims in our wake. If you have ever apologized, what are you acknowledging? That your sin has victims, that you are an oppressor and a victimizer. The God of the Bible loves victims. Look at what God says in Genesis 7:11—"The Earth is filled with violence"—and in Genesis 7:13—"For the Earth is filled with violence." What is God saying? He is saying, "I must act. I am personally involved with this world. I hear the cry for justice. How can I not answer it?"

If you want a God who is there, who is present and intimately involved, then you must have a God who cares about victims. He must bring judgment to the victimizer. The word that is used here for the word "sorry" and "regret" is often translated "to console oneself," but another translation is "to have compassion for another," so when the Lord is saying, "I am sorry I made man," one way of reading that would be "The Lord looks at the damage being caused and says to the victim, 'I am sorry I have made the one who is victimizing you. I am sorry I have made the oppressor. I am sorry this has happened.'" God is saying, "I see what they are doing and I hate what they are doing; I have compassion."

When tragedy happens, we ask, "Where is God?" We want the pastor to preach a sermon answering the question "Where is God?" because we ask, "How could this kind of evil happen and God not do something about it?" But then we hear that God is going to judge us and he has a standard that we cannot meet and we say, "I do not believe in that kind of God. I believe in a loving God." Do you see how those two statements do not go together? Which is it? Does God care about judging and punishing evil, or does God simply say, "I am Mr. Love, so I do not judge anyone or anything"?

Do you see how neither one of those extremes helps you? If God only judges, we are doomed. Everything we do is in his sight; everything we think, everything we say, and everything we do not say is in his sight. But if God is only love, we are equally doomed because that means there is no hope for the victim or oppressed. If we do not believe in God, we are left with the dilemma of believing that evil is simply natural. We do not have any kind of answer for evil. The best answer for evil is the biblical God.

Miroslav Volf, an Eastern European theologian who grew up in the Bosnian–Serbian conflict, wrote a book called *Exclusion and Embrace*. In it, he writes about violence and judgment and how we perceive them. He writes:

> In a world of violence, it would not be worthy of God not to wield the sword; if God were not angry at injustice and deception, and did not make the final end of violence, God would not be worthy of our worship. ... My thesis ... will be unpopular with many Christians, especially theologians in the West. To the person inclined to dismiss it, I suggest

imagining that you are delivering a lecture in a war zone. ...
Among your listeners are peoples whose cities and villages
have first been plundered, then burned and leveled to the
ground, whose daughters and sisters have been raped, whose
fathers and brothers have had their throats slit. ... Soon you
will discover that it takes the quiet of suburban [life to
believe the opposite]. (pp. 303–304)

He is saying, "If you grew up where I grew up, you have to believe in
a God of judgment."

When you know you are wrong, what do you want? You want mercy.
But when others are wrong, what do you want? You want justice. But
do you know what others want when you wrong them? Justice. You
cannot understand the Bible, you can never understand Jesus, until you
are willing to acknowledge that not only should God judge the world
but he should also judge you.

The biblical story of the flood tells us that judgment delayed is not
judgment denied. The whole time Noah is building the ark, everyone
is saying, "No big deal. What is going on? No worries." Jesus would say
in Matthew 24 that Noah's contemporaries were eating and drinking,
celebrating and living life while Noah was building an ark. Do not
confuse God's patience with God's ignorance. The flood does come.

What Does the Ark Tell Us about God?

Look at what God says to Noah in Genesis 6:13: "I am determined to
make an end of all flesh for the Earth is filled with violence through
them. Behold, I will destroy them with the Earth. Make yourself an
ark of gofer wood and make rooms in the ark." He is saying, "Yes, I am
going to judge the earth, but that is not all I am doing. I am doing
something other than that. Noah, build a big boat." Yes, he floods the
earth, but the same God who floods the earth says, "Build a boat and
put some rooms in it."

Every time God has brought judgment, he has brought an ark. This is the first physical ark we have seen; it is not the first metaphorical ark we have seen. Adam and Eve eat from the tree, and God shows up and makes loincloths for them. Cain is thinking about killing his brother, and God shows up to warn him. Cain kills his brother, and God shows up and puts a mark on Cain so nobody else will kill him. God is more than a judge; he is an ark builder, too. Every time there is judgment, there is a way of escape.

Not only is God more than a judge but he is passionate about making things new. God is personally invested in this world; he is not letting the world go to hell in a handbasket. God made the earth, and the earth is good. It is not the earth's fault we have messed it up. God is passionate about this world. Only Christianity says salvation is not an escape from this world but that salvation is a restoration of this world.

God says, in Genesis 6:17, "For behold, I will bring a flood of waters upon the Earth to destroy all flesh in which is the breath of life under Heaven." That is a very important phrase. Everything that is on the earth shall die. We then read, in Genesis 6:19, "And the waters prevailed so mightily on the Earth that all the high mountains under the whole heavens were covered." And in Genesis 7:22, we read, "Everything on the dry land in whose nostrils was the breath of life died." Why is there an emphasis on the breath of life? Why is it important that we know the water was over the mountains? In Genesis 1:2, what covered the land? Water. This is a re-creation. God is re-covering everything with water. He is starting over. Instead of Adam and Eve, God has Noah and his family in the ark. Instead of making animals all over again, he places them on a boat. God is making things new. Even though the world is evil and God floods the earth, he has not given up on it. He is simply going back to Genesis 1 and saying, "Let us do this again." God is passionate about this planet. He is passionate about the people on Earth and passionate about making things new.

When the waters recede, it is a new Earth. All the evil is gone. All the contaminants are gone. There is a new humanity on the ark. When Noah and his family get off, Genesis 9:1 says, "And God blessed Noah and his sons and said to them 'Be fruitful and multiply and fill the Earth.'" Why is that important? God is starting over. This is a re-creation.

Grace is the instrument God uses to make things new. Grace is the unmerited favor of God. This is shown in Genesis 6:8: "But Noah found favor [or grace] in the eyes of the Lord." God then says in verse 18, "But I will establish my covenant with you, my promise to you, and you shall come into the ark, you, your sons, your wife and your sons' wives with you." You know why you get instructions on how the ark was built? It is God's grace to Noah saying, "Because I want you to survive, I am going to give you all the things you need to survive. I am going to give you grace."

If this passage is about grace, why does the author talk about Noah's righteousness? First of all, the first instance of Noah's righteousness that you see comes at what theologians would call the heading of a passage, which means the start of the passage. Genesis 6:9 says, "Noah was a blameless man." How do we know that Noah was a blameless man? Because when he receives the grace of God and God says, "Build a boat," he builds a boat. That is the only thing we know about Noah: He receives God's grace and he builds a boat. Listen to what Hebrews 11:7 says about Noah's righteousness: "By faith, Noah being warned by God concerning events as yet unseen, in reverent fear constructed an ark for the saving of his household. By this he condemned the world and became an heir of the righteousness that comes by faith." What does the writer of Hebrews say about how we are to understand Noah's righteousness? We understand Noah's righteousness as a response to the grace of God by faith.

The whole Bible teaches us that we cannot hope to make ourselves righteous and then ask for grace. Instead, the Bible invites us to receive grace and be made righteous by grace. God wants to make this world new. How is he going to make this world new? Not through a political campaign, a social campaign, or an economic campaign. He is going to make the world new through grace.

Finally, we see that God's grace provides a means of escape from his judgment. We have a multidimensional God bringing judgment but also providing a means of escape from the judgment. In the story of Noah, there are two types of people. There are those who say, "I do not need grace," and those who say, "I will build a boat, because I need grace." That is the only difference here. You do not have good people and bad people; you have grace-receiving people and grace-ignoring people.

What does the flood tell us about God? That God is a good God who judges wicked people who oppress and hurt people. This is bad news for us—we are those people. What does the ark tell us about God? It tells us that the same God who brings judgment always provides a means of escape. And the way we access that means of escape is through grace.

Did the Flood Work?

If you read the story of Noah as a story of God trying to get rid of all the bad people, then the flood did not work. One preacher says three things went on the boat with Noah: his family, his animals, and sin. How do we know that? As soon as Noah gets off the boat, he builds a vineyard, gets drunk, and lies around naked. If you read the story of Noah as God getting rid of all the bad people, you see he forgot one—Noah. Instead, we are to understand the flood is pointing to a greater judgment: a flood to come. You may ask, "Where do you get this from?"

In the Gospels, Jesus says this about the flood: "For as were the days of Noah, so will be the coming of the Son of Man. For as in those days before the flood, they were eating and drinking, marrying and given in marriage, until the day when Noah entered the ark, and they were unaware until the flood came and swept them all away, so will be the coming of the Son of Man" (Matthew 24:37–39). The Bible is talking about Jesus coming and judging the world.

This points us to the fact that God must judge. It is a living monument to remind us that God is loving but that his love requires judgment. His love does not excuse judgment; it requires judgment. Jesus is saying, "Just as it was then, so it is going to be for all of us."

Just like in the days of Noah, people in Jesus's time thought they could do whatever they wanted and get away with it. They thought God was absent and was not going to do anything because he must have given up on the world. Jesus says, "It was not that way for them, and it is not that way for us." The first eleven chapters of Genesis establish a pattern of behavior, not just for humans but also for God, who says to us all, "If you turn away from God, you will be judged." We have all turned away from God, so we all will be judged. You cannot understand Christianity, you cannot understand the Bible, and you cannot understand Jesus unless you are willing to say, "I deserve the judgment of God." The first step is to admit you are fundamentally flawed and should be held responsible for it.

If, every time God judges, he provides an escape, what is our way of escape? We think we can escape if we are good. If we come into this saying, "I am all right. I am okay," we will never get anywhere with Christianity. When we begin our relationship with God that way, we will never get anywhere.

What do we see in the ark? On the basis of Noah's righteousness, his family is saved. Noah obeys, and as a result, his family is saved. Noah is in the ark because he heard and obeyed. Everybody else is in the ark because Noah heard and obeyed.

In doing this act of obedience for others, Noah points to Jesus. The Bible tells us that our only hope in escaping the judgment of God is not that we become super-righteous people but rather that we pin our hopes to a greater Noah whose obedience provides the means of escape for us. The Bible says that Jesus is the greater Noah because on the cross he is building our means of escape from the judgment of God. When Jesus comes to Earth and he lives a sinless life, that is how he builds the boat. Every temptation he resists and every righteous act he does becomes a nail and a board in the ark of our rescue. On the cross, as he dies for our sins, he is inviting us to climb on board his goodness in order that we might survive the flood of God's judgment. You cannot be both right and righteous. You have to pick one. You have to say, "My hope is in my goodness," or "My hope is in the goodness of Jesus Christ."

Peter says the same thing about the flood: "Baptism, which corresponds to [being brought safely through the flood] now saves you. Not as removal of dirt from the body, but as an appeal to God for a good conscience through the resurrection of Jesus Christ" (1 Peter 3:21–22). Peter is saying Noah's family's only hope when the rain started falling was that Noah had really heard from God. And our only hope when the rain of God's judgment begins to fall in our lives is that Jesus Christ and what he has done is our good conscience. God created a way to give us Jesus's righteousness and to give Jesus our imperfection at the cross.

We have a God of judgment and a God of grace. How do we reconcile these two? The only way to reconcile them is on the cross of Jesus Christ, where God's judgment is being poured out and his way of escape is being lifted up. Do you trust in your own rightness? That is like walking out in Noah's day with an umbrella; it will work for a little while, but in the end, you will be swept away. Your only hope is to say, "I am not good, but I know someone who is. I did not hear from God the way Jesus did, but just like Noah's family, I have climbed up on the boat." Jesus told his followers, "In my father's house there are many rooms. I go to prepare a place for you" (John 14:2). You know what that sounds like? It sounds like God saying, "Noah, build a boat and make many rooms." Your only hope is that there is a room for you on the ark of Jesus's death and resurrection.

Chapter 7

Self or Significance

Genesis 11:1–9

The story of the tower of Babel is an interesting one, particularly in the way God reacts to what the people are doing. God sounds a little scared. He looks very reactionary and you wonder, why in the world is God reacting this way to people building a city and a tower? Why is there this language of God's concern, and why does he launch a preemptive strike on the people at Babel? Why would God respond and react this way? And how does that bear on our lives here? When we read this story, we find the people who are building the city of Babel and its tower in the center are very like us. What God says about them and what God does to them is relevant for us because these people are like us. To show that, I aim to display where we agree with God, where we disagree with God, and why we know he is right.

Where We Agree with God

Until the middle part of Genesis 11:4, everything these people are doing is actually wonderful. It is in line with the teaching of the Bible.

The people at Babel have lofty aspirations. They are trying to build a city because God has hard-wired humanity to have a sense, value, and worth of its own significance. You and I should wake up in the morning saying, "What I do matters. I need to find purpose. I need to find meaning. I need to be significant." The Bible says these thoughts are because God has hard-wired people. When God created the world, he created a place where human beings could flourish, then he rested on the seventh day. God took a Sabbath rest, and that day has not ended; it is ongoing. God has created the world, and he has given it to humanity, and by resting, he is saying, "Shape it and mold it. Take care of it. Build things. Build cities. Develop technology. Start families. Have lots of babies. That is what it means to be human."

In other words, what the Bible is saying is all things on this planet have meaning and purpose. The tree, the squirrel, and the wind all have meaning. All these biological and physiological things have meaning and value, but only humans have a sense of their meaning and value. Only people wake up in the morning and say, "Am I going to do anything today? Am I going to get an education? Am I going to start my career? Am I going to date this person? Are we going to start having children? Are we going to start having more children?" The people at the tower of Babel have the same sense of significance that so many of us have. They have woken up and said, "You know what? Let us do something significant. Let us do something lofty. Let us build a city." The Bible says that is absolutely what humans should be doing.

In Genesis 1:28, God says, "Fill the Earth and subdue it, and have dominion." Inherent in this verse is a command to build and do things so every one of us not only is significant but feels significant. This edict from God stands over and against the naturalistic worldview that says if you wake up in the morning and say, "I need meaning. I need purpose," those thoughts are mirages. The Bible says you are an image bearer of God meant to be significant.

Not only are humans significant, but life is the unfolding of that significance. Life is about uncovering, discovering, unfolding that significance in the world. People are getting together; they are building cities. Men and women are coming together. When you build a city, do you not need all types of people? You need architects, city planners, construction workers, skilled tradespeople, and people to encourage you. You need diversity. The Bible says all human beings are significant. We all bear God's image, and yet there is a nuanced difference to our significance. We are not significant in a monolithic sense. We are not significant because we have hands and feet and are human. We are significant because we bear God's image and we all bear it differently. We have all different kinds of people, and they are all necessary. Only the Bible says that not only are human beings significant but that each is uniquely significant. The Bible is saying, "Yes! That is all good."

The unfolding of our unique significance is a communal project. We are not all set on individual trajectories to go find our own good. Throughout Genesis, the Bible is saying that human beings are called to subdue and fill and multiply; it is a communal thing. Try being fruitful and multiplying by yourself. We can't; we do it together. The same is true with shaping and molding. Have you ever noticed how exciting it is to be a part of a mission or a movement? Hard-wired in each of us is a desire to be a part of something bigger than our individual lives.

Not only are we significant, not only is life about unfolding the significance, not only is that a communal project, but the city is a focal point of all these things. Where do we go to uncover our significance and to do it communally? We go to the city. The city is not the only place where this happens, but it is a primary place where this happens. Throughout history, many people have read the Bible and come away saying, "Cities are bad." So far, we have seen two cities, the city of Lamech and now Babel, but cities are good and cities need to be good. Cities are simply places where humans gather. The city is a place where we fulfill our mandate from God and we do it safely. Within a city, there is this idea of communal safety, coming together in order to be protected.

Some would say the city is primarily a place for the individual. The communal is not important; the individual is important, with his or her individual rights, individual liberties. These thoughts have led to things like people leaving the city, developing suburbs—high-priced suburbs that you can live in only if you make a certain amount of money, with gated communities and country clubs. These things are not evil, but they are born out of this idea that what is best about the city is that it gives an individual platform and there is no communal aspect. Others say the city is for community and it is not for the individual good; it is for the corporate good. The Bible says both of those ideas are wrong. If you show up to the city saying, "Make me great!" you have missed the point of the city. If you show up to the city and say, "Do not worry about the individual; it is all about the community. Human beings are not significant individually; they are just significant corporately," you have missed the point of the city, the Bible says. The city is a place for both of these things to happen.

People are typically going to the city for one of two reasons. Some go in order to uncover their own significance. This is true of most students. You come and you are studying great things and you are going to do great things. You have come to the city to uncover your significance. Even if you are not a student, you have come to start a career. You have gotten the first job and the trajectory you have planned for yourself, and the city is going to be a place where you are going to make a name for yourself. Others go to the city to make the city great. They talk about things like sustainability and building communities and neighborhoods that last. The Bible is saying that both of those things are true of what it means to be human and what it means to be in the city.

Here is where we agree with God: You feel significant because you are significant. You feel as though you have individual significance because you do. And if you feel as though your individual significance needs to be plugged into the corporate significance, you are right! And if you feel the city is a good place to do that, you are absolutely right.

Where Do We Disagree with God?

If that is where we agree with God, where do we disagree with God? Look at what the people say in Genesis 11:4: "Come, let us build ourselves a city. And a tower with its top in the heavens. And let us make a name for ourselves, lest we be dispersed over the face of the whole Earth." What is driving them to build the city is the problem. It is not that the city is bad. It is not that being significant is bad. It is not that working together is bad. It is their motivations that are bad.

Without God, the human search for significance becomes self-exaltation. You see it here as the people proclaim, "Let us make a name for ourselves. Let us build a city that, centuries from now, people will be in and they will remember us. Let us build a tower up to the heavens." Most scholars believe that what they are building is a ziggurat, the spiral building that goes all the way up to the heavens. In the ancient cultures, they believed that the higher you got, the more leverage or more bargaining power you had with the gods and the more likely the gods were to respond to you positively because you were closer to them. These people are seeking significance neither in God nor from God. They seek it apart from God. Even worse than apart from God, they are seeking significance over and against God. They are seeking to be God themselves. If you can build a tower to the heavens, if you can climb it, and if you can say, "God, you must give me what I want because I have done this," then you are, in essence, God. If God has to bark at your orders, then you are God and he is the minion.

Not only are they seeking to make a name for themselves, not only are they trying to be God, they are actually directly rebelling against God. In Genesis 2, God says, "Spread out. Have children and spread out and cover the earth." In Genesis 9, he says to Noah, "Spread out and cover the earth." But here, what do they say? Why are they building a city? "So that we will not be dispersed." So what sounds like safety, what sounds like security, is actually rebellion against God. The city is turning into a place of self-exaltation. We are only nine chapters away from God giving humanity the massive task of filling the Earth, but we are already taking all the tools God has given us and doing the opposite of what we're supposed to do. We are setting ourselves up as God.

Not only without God does a search for significance become self-exaltation, but self-exaltation quickly becomes oppression. When life becomes all about me, inevitably, I oppress other people. Inevitably, I exert my power and influence in a way that crushes and harms. Over time, if we seek to exalt ourselves, we end up hurting one another. When you think along these lines, then what God says in response to the building project makes absolute sense. "Behold they are one people. They have all one language. And this is only the beginning of what they will do. Nothing that they propose to do will now be impossible" (Genesis 11:5–6).

To be clear, God is not afraid of cities. Guess where the Bible ends in Revelation 21? A city. He is not afraid of their architecture, construction, and togetherness. Rather, God has seen this story before with Cain. Unlike Cain, where we had one family saying, "Let me make a name for myself," and doing the limited amount of oppression that one family can do, here you have multiple people leveraging all they have to make a name for themselves—and God knows, over time, a city built for self-exaltation becomes a place of oppression.

Conservatives say, "Let us get out of the city," and they leave behind the shell of the city. Many people who really need to stay in the city, serve the city, and change the city move out of the city and leave a vacuum in their place, so in comes the liberal saying, "Oh I told you, you have to love the city." But let us think about this. What is the most liberal expression of communal living? It is communism. Have you ever read *Animal Farm*? The pigs say, "Let us get rid of the farmer and we will all have value and we will all have significance"—and that works, right up until the point where the pigs decide they have more value and more significance than the other animals. The pigs rule the farm and turn into that which they despise. Whether you are right-leaning or left-leaning, it does not matter. Inevitably, when you seek to exalt your own self or the corporate self, it leads to oppression. God knows that is where this city is going, and he intervenes.

Apart from God, the search for significance becomes self-exaltation and will lead to oppression. It will also lead to self-oppression. These people give their lives to building the city. They put all their time and energy into building the city and its tower and making a name for themselves, and in one verse, the Bible says, "And from there the LORD dispersed them over the face of all the Earth" (Genesis 11:9b) and they ceased building the city. These people have given their lives to something that, in the end, does not last. No one is going to remember their city. No one is going to remember their names. When we eliminate God from the equation and we wake up in the morning and say, "I want to be significant," we have nowhere to appeal for that significance. We have to go out and earn our significance by competing with each other, by getting the job, or by getting the part at the expense of someone else. We elevate ourselves at the cost of each other. When we wake up in the morning and say, "I want to be significant," and our neighbor does the same, the Bible says, over time, someone has to give.

If you seek to make yourself significant, you are successful at it, and you spend your life thinking you have made it, eventually, you die and everything you have done goes to nothingness, like the tower of Babel. Even if you are successful, in the end, what did you really accomplish? When people make names for themselves, they do it at great cost. They do it at the cost of their families; they do it at the cost of their spouses; and they do it at the cost of personal health. It is not wrong to build a city, but if the point of building a city is to make a name for yourself, then ultimately building the city is pointless. You are going to lose yourself. It is not wrong to have a career. It is not wrong to have a family. It is not wrong to have a trajectory that you would like life to go on. But if from these things, you are going to get your significance apart from God, you are only a step or two away from being destroyed. Or if you spend your whole life trying to be significant, only you do not make it, you will spend your whole life feeling like a disappointment and living with regret.

The Bible says either one of those will crush you. So, when we agree with God that we are significant, that we have meaning, and we find it corporately, the city can be a place of meaning. We disagree with God when we believe that meaning is ultimately to make much of ourselves. God disagrees with you not just because he is God and you are not, but because God loves you and he knows the end result of trying to live a life to make much of yourself: Such a life is to be wasted in the end, even after success, or to be crushed in failure.

How Do We Know God Is Right?

We agree with God and we disagree with God, yet how do we know God is right? First, we know he is right because human history tells us that is true. What great movement has lasted? Even if it is successful, it ends. All these movements and civilizations come and go, and they do not last. We also know that God is right because individual lives tell us the story. If making a name for yourself financially was what life was about, if you could get meaning and purpose from that, then every time I found a rich person, I would find a happy person. If having a great family or a great marriage really completed life, every person who had kids and every person who was married would be happy. But that is not the case. Human history and individual lives tell us that it is not through self-exaltation that we find significance.

Then where do we find it? We can look to Genesis 12:1–3: "Now the LORD said to Abram, go from your country and your kindred and your father's house to the land that I will show you and I will make of you a great nation and I will bless you and make your name great so that you will be a blessing and in you all the families of the Earth shall be blessed." This is being said in the rubble of the tower of Babel. He destroys the project and then he speaks to a guy named Abram. People go to build the city and say, "Let us make our name great." God says to Abram, "I am going to make your name great." How? He tells you. "I am going to make you into a great nation. I am going to bless you and make your name great. You will be a great blessing. In you all the families of the earth shall be blessed." How does God fulfill his promise to Abram (Abraham)? Through Jesus. Jesus is a descendant of Abraham. The Gospel of Matthew (chapter 1) and the Gospel of Luke (chapter 3) will take you all the way, in a genealogy, from Adam to Abraham to Jesus. Luke says that it is through Jesus that this promise given to Abraham to become a great nation will be fulfilled.

Jesus comes to earth as the truly righteous man. He lives a righteous life that you and I could not live, and yet he goes to the cross and suffers as though he was building Babel. Jesus is the opposite of us. In Mark 10:45, Jesus says, "I have come not to be served, but to serve." You and I wake up in the morning asking, "How can I make a name for myself?" Jesus woke up asking not how he could make a name for himself but "How can I do exactly what it is that God wants me to do?" And yet when he goes to the cross, he is punished like he is us—a builder of the tower of Babel. He is punished for our sin, for our desire to self-exalt, for the oppression that you and I bring about through our self-exaltation.

Jesus, on the cross, asks, "My God, My God, why have you forsaken me?" (Matthew 27:46). God's silence says, "I am forsaking you because it is what these people deserve." And when Jesus rises from the dead, God takes his righteousness, his sinlessness, his God-exaltation, and gives it to us. When you come to faith in Jesus, you are saying, "My hope is that God has punished Jesus for my sin and is rewarding me for Jesus's righteousness." That is why Christians talk so much about grace.

Going a step further, what happens after you have come to faith in Jesus? God reverses what he did at the tower of Babel. In Acts 2, Peter begins to preach on the day of Pentecost and everybody hears his words in their own language. What is being reversed in Acts 2? Multiple languages serving as barriers. Not only does he reverse the languages, but God also reverses our insignificance. In 1 Peter 2:9–10, we are told that all people who come to faith in Jesus are made into a significant people: "But you are a chosen race, a royal priesthood, a holy nation, a people for his own possession. . . . Once, you were not a people, but now you are God's people." God has given us a new identity.

Finally, in Revelation 21, we become inhabitants of the new and better city. God is not an enemy of cities; he is not an enemy of community; and he is not an enemy of significance. Instead, what God has said is that if you and I seek significance apart from him, we will always exalt ourselves, we will always oppress others, and we will ultimately oppress ourselves. But if we seek significance through the name of Jesus, we can have all these things that we are hard-wired to want without hurting anyone and without hurting ourselves. The city coming down from heaven in Revelation 21 is the true Babel. It is the new and better city, not with a tower that reaches up to the heavens but rather with a king who comes from the heavens. This city is not one of ascension but condescension.

If you want meaning and purpose, do you have to set that aside to become a Christian? No. What you have to set aside is the belief that what will ultimately make you happy is to make much of yourself. God scrambles the plans at Babel and from the wreckage pulls out one guy and says, "I am going to do something great through you," and that one guy, as we will see throughout the Bible, eventually leads us to Jesus.

If you are a Christian, you might not wake up in the morning and ask, "What can I do to advance my name? What can I do to make much of myself? Life is about my plans, my dream, my vision, my effort, my success, and my name." Rather, you are saying, "That used to be my life. Now I am seeking all of those things, but in a way to make a name for Jesus." To be a Christian is not to stop being an engineer or to stop studying engineering, but it is ultimately to find your significance not in the label or the paycheck. To become a Christian is not to say, "I am no longer a father. I am no longer a mother. I am no longer a husband or wife." Rather, it is to say, "I do not get my meaning from those things; I get my meaning from what God has done for me and from what he is doing through me in Jesus."

As a culture, we talk a lot about restoration. This, we believe, is our hope. But our hope is not that we make much of the individual or of the community over and against the individual. The hope for cities is that people like you and me learn to find our significance in what God is doing in the better city. Our hope is that we can be set free from self-exaltation, set free from being oppressed or needing to oppress, and that we begin to love people.

The Bible says you can sum up all of Scripture by loving God with all your heart, soul, and mind and by loving your neighbor as yourself (Matthew 22:36–40). If you eliminate loving God from that equation and you say, "I'm just going to love myself and love my neighbor," you are crawling into a bottomless hole from which you will never climb out. You will live a whole life of loving yourself, but you will never find time to actually get around to loving your neighbor. But when you come to know and love God, when you get your significance not from what you can do but from what God has done for you, you are set free to love yourself, not because you achieve but because what God has said about you is true, and then you can get around to loving your neighbor.

How do we love God? By turning to the person and work of Jesus Christ, who came down for our good and the good of all the people who live in the city with us. We commit to finding our significance in Jesus, the true and better city and the true and better king.

Chapter 8

Promise or Performance

Genesis 11:10–12:3

Abraham is a very significant historic figure. The world's three largest monotheistic religions—Islam, Judaism, and Christianity—trace their origins back to him. All of Genesis 1–11 has been leading us up to this moment when we meet Abraham. With this in mind, let us consider three things while reading Abraham's story: the wrong place to go for hope, the right place to go for hope, and what happens when you find hope.

The Wrong Place to Go for Hope

The story of Genesis 1–11 tells us that the wrong place to go for hope is inward, to look in the mirror so to speak. Looking outward is just as dangerous, to look to some kind of corporate project or to get a bunch of people together and make plans to change the world. In fact, if you read the story of Genesis 1–11, you will see two things right off the bat. First, things go wrong for us when we become disconnected from God. In Genesis 3, we see Adam and Eve living in the garden, a perfect place for human flourishing. They are given a great purpose, but when they decide they can flourish without God, they become disconnected from God and are forced out of the garden into a world of destruction. Second, we see there is no way that we, on our own effort, can get back to being connected with God. In fact, Genesis 1–11 reads as a decline in man. It is a moral devolution, a regression.

We start with humanity knowing God, loving God, and serving God. In Genesis 3, Adam and Eve decide it is better to be without God and to live in a world where they know good and evil, rather than in a world where they know only good and trust God to distinguish between the two. They eat the fruit and they rebel against God. In Genesis 4, Cain's religious hypocrisy leads to murder. The descendant of Cain, Lamech, is king of the city. He oppresses women, takes multiple wives, and treats women as objects. He kills a young boy just for bruising him.

In Genesis 6, we see that this very same city becomes a place of oppression of all kinds: political, social, gender, and familial oppression. Our inability to appease God leads to a flood in Genesis 7. People are drowned and die as a part of the judgment. In Genesis 9, we see that even good people like Noah have secrets and dark corners. As Noah gets off the boat, he builds a vineyard, gets drunk, rolls around naked, and babbles like a fool. In Genesis 11, people come together and decide to build a city to be like God—and God, with three words, destroys that city, showing us that we are not God.

It is not until we get to Genesis 11:10 that we get to the line of Shem. It was Shem's lineage that Noah said God would bless (Genesis 9:25–27). As we read the line of Shem, we find that Abram's father, Terah, is named after a moon god. Abram and his family live in Ur of the Chaldeans, a place of lunar worship. Even the handpicked people of God have resorted to worshipping something as insignificant as the moon.

Genesis 1–11 is telling us that human effort will never fix our world. When you become introspective enough to look in the mirror and say, "Many of the problems in my life are of my own doing, and even the ones that were not my fault, I have simply amplified with my own mistakes," you will begin to understand these passages. No matter where you look in Genesis, you cannot find one human to put your hope in. The Bible says that you and I not only cannot fix the world but also cannot fix even ourselves.

You know that is true for two reasons. If you follow human history, you will see countless ideas for how to do government, how to relate to each other socially, how to structure cities, and how to build the perfect society, yet we still cannot find this perfection. But if you are honest with yourself, you know we can't find the solution to the world's problems because we do not have the solution for our own problems. Genesis 1–11 tells us time and time again that when you are looking for hope, you will not find it in yourself. You are not going to find hope in human effort, in a politician, in a professor, in a career, or in a family. Why? Because, as Genesis 1–11 tells us, ultimately, the problem is that we are disconnected from God.

We cannot reconnect ourselves to God through human effort. In Genesis 3, Adam and Eve are the ones who separate humanity from God, but you and I perpetuate that separation *daily* in the choices we make, in the things we do. You must understand this idea that human effort, your own morality, will never put you back together, in order to understand the Bible. Genesis 1–11 tells us over and over again, in different ways and through many examples, that we will never find solutions by looking inward.

The Right Place to Go for Hope

If inside is the wrong place to go, where is the right place to go? Unlike the humans in Genesis who have been unable to keep their promises, God has the complete opposite performance record. God always shows up, and he always does what he says he is going to do, in spite of humanity's imperfection.

In Genesis 1, God creates a good world for human flourishing, a perfect environment that is completely fine-tuned for human life. In Genesis 2, God makes a helper for Adam. Adam is not big enough for the job God has given Adam to do, so God gives Eve to Adam as the perfect complement. In Genesis 3, God warns them that if they eat from a certain tree, they are going to die. They eat from the tree, and God keeps his promise, Adam and Eve do die, but even then, God makes another promise. He promises to send someone to fix this. In spite of Adam and Eve's rebellion, God is there, keeping his word and showing grace. In Genesis 4, Cain murders Abel, yet God shows grace in warning Cain and after Cain has murdered Abel by protecting him from others.

Throughout Genesis, God preserves a line of people. In Genesis 6, the whole world is chaos, but Noah finds grace in the eyes of the Lord. God is faithful, keeping the story of human history going by preserving the line of Noah and Shem. In Genesis 6 and 7, God shows grace to Noah's family and rescues them from the flood. In Genesis 11, God keeps the city of Babel from being built because he has already seen the oppression of Lamech in Genesis 4. He knows that unchecked cities become cities of oppression, so he keeps another city of oppression from being built. Everywhere you look in Genesis 1–11, you see humans failing. Everywhere you look, humans are rebelling against God. But just as visible is a faithful, promise-keeping God. Genesis 1–11 can be summed up by this statement: "We are not faithful, but God is. You cannot do this, but God can. You cannot trust yourself, but you can trust God."

God makes a promise to us in Genesis 3 that his faithfulness will be to our benefit. God promises to send a seed to rescue humanity, yet by Genesis 11, the people from whom the promised seed is supposed to come are worshipping the moon. It appears that God has made a promise but human inability is getting in the way of that promise.

This human inability is even communicated in the two genealogies preceding chapter 11. Both of these genealogies, found in Genesis 5 and 10, give ten generations; however, utilizing a poetic device, the genealogy of chapter 10 includes only eight names, thus intentionally leaving off two names. By doing this, the author communicates two things: first, the reality that human inability cannot stop the promise of God, and second, that another two names are coming. One spot is reserved for Isaac, the son of Abraham. Who does the tenth spot belong to in the Genesis 11 genealogy? We could plug a lot of names in there, including Jacob, Joseph, Judah, and Moses. Instead, the real name we are plugging in is Jesus. Abraham has Isaac, the son of promise, but the last son is Jesus. Jesus is the tenth man of Genesis 11. He is the one for whom we are waiting. The Bible is saying that if we look inward, we will never find hope, but God's promise is that he will send someone through Abraham, and that is Jesus.

This is why Matthew begins his gospel with the genealogy. He goes all the way from Abraham to David, from David to Jesus. He is saying the son promised to Abraham was Isaac but the great-great-great, great grandson promised to deliver the world is Jesus.

The Gospel message of Christianity is not that we look inwardly for hope but rather that we look to God and how he overcomes our inability through Jesus Christ. Everyone who comes from Adam keeps messing up, but not the God-man, Jesus Christ. God overcame human inability by becoming a man and living the life we could not live, then dying on the cross to pay the price for the life we have actually lived. On the cross, an exchange is taking place. Jesus's life is credited to those who look to the cross in faith, and their sin is credited to Jesus.

The problem with humanity is that we are disconnected from God. When we are disconnected from God, we have no choice but to become our own god, and we set out oppressing each other. The answer to our problem is to be reconnected with God, but we can't reconnect with him on our own, so God became a man to live the life that would reconnect us with God. On the cross, Jesus is grabbing God and grabbing man and bringing them together, reconciling them.

So many of us fit into one of two categories, and both are problematic. Those in the first category hear the Gospel of Jesus Christ and do not embrace it as their hope. Those in the second group hear the Gospel and believe it for eternity but do not let it affect their day-to-day lives at all. The Gospel becomes eternally essential to avoid the judgment of God but becomes practically irrelevant. For some, the problem is rooted in unbelief. For others who claim to be Christians, how do we know that we really are living a Gospel-centered life and not one in which Christ is practically irrelevant?

There is a way you can know that you are understanding the Gospel correctly. It is to find hope in the Gospel and to trust simply in God's promise for your identity. In the Genesis 11 genealogy, we see that Abram comes from Terah, a moon worshipper. Abram is a pagan who belongs to a pagan family. He is just a normal guy living his life when God shows up. Abram is not looking for God; he is not reading about God; and he is not having an existential crisis. God simply shows up.

You know that you have embraced the Gospel if you can trace your life back to a moment when God showed up. To embrace the Gospel is to meet God, not because you were looking for him but because he showed up. Abram responds to the gracious, undeserved, and unexpected intrusion of God into his life. That is how the embrace begins. We know that we have begun to embrace the Gospel when we see that God has shown up in our lives and he has done something we were not looking for and it changes us. You can listen to all sorts of sermons, but unless you hear the call of God, sermons are just sermons. When the call of God shows up, you begin to trust it as the promise of your identity.

What Happens When We Find Hope

There are two ways you can know that your whole identity is in the Gospel. The first is rooted in performance. What happens if you mess up? If you read the story of Abram, you will find that he messes up a lot. He falls into some mistakes, and he runs into others, but the whole time, Abram keeps running toward the promise of God. Abram's relationship with God is not one of performance but of promise. The basis of their relationship wasn't Abram's promise to God but God's promise to Abram. You have really grasped the Gospel when you get off the roller-coaster ride of "I feel close to God when I'm good. I feel far away from God when I am bad." When you ride that roller coaster, it is evident that you are not grasping the Gospel. The Gospel says the same thing that God says to Abram: "Go. I am going to do this." God says to us in the Gospel, "Go, I have already done this."

So many are on this roller coaster of performance. So many say, "I do not feel close to God because I have not been reading my Bible." The Gospel is not that you put your confidence in reading the Bible. The Gospel is that you put your confidence in knowing that what you could not and would not do, Jesus has done. In the upcoming chapters of Genesis, Abram will fall headlong into one mistake after another, and so will you. The way to know that you have grasped the Gospel is that you do not hide from God when your performance is low. Instead, you run to God when your performance is low and say, "My performance is low! I am so grateful you have given me another's performance to trust."

What we call obedience, Abram would call the excitement of discovering what following God looks like. One way of understanding this passage is to think of Abram as a very obedient guy. But he is not that obedient. Another way of understanding this passage is that Abram was very excited to see how God was going to pull his promise off. In the Gospel, obedience is not a means of earning God but of discovering God. It is a way in which we see how God is going to do something.

If you are single and you meet someone at a party and you are both interested in each other and the other person says to you, "Hey, meet me tonight at nine o'clock," you are obeying them when you show up that night. We do not think of it as obedience since we would be excited about discovering the other person. For Abram, moving forward was not about obeying God, it was about discovering what God was going to do. It was about believing that God is a promise maker and promise keeper. We do what God asks us to do not because we earn anything by doing it. Instead, when we do what he says, we believe he is going to do something great.

The way you know you are holding fast to the Gospel is when you know that your status is bound up in Jesus's obedience but you want to do the things God calls you to do because you believe that God has great a purpose for you. In doing what God has called you to do, you discover what those great things are. If you relate to God on the basis of dos and don'ts, you will never sustain a relationship with God. One, because your default is to disobey, as we have seen since the garden. Two, because you will beat yourself up with your guilt and shame. But if you say, "By obeying God, I discover God," you will be like Abram, a believer primarily, who will become a doer.

You will know that you have prized the Gospel when your identity does not rise or fall with your moral progress but with Jesus's life and death. You prize the Gospel when listening to and heeding the voice of God becomes discovery, not obedience. To find the Gospel is to walk away from any other kind of identity. Genesis 12:1–2 is about Abram leaving everything that would have identified him as Abram. God takes away his family, his homeland, and his religion. Why? Because God is washing Genesis 3–11 off of Abram. God says, "I'm taking you somewhere, and in order to get there, we have to get rid of this. We have got to strip you of these things."

To know that you have begun to embrace the Gospel is to look in the mirror and say, "I used to find hope in my looks, in my bank account, in my career, in being the best spouse or having the best-behaved children. Now those things do not define me. My hope is in the promise of God."

This does not mean you abandon all ambition. The difference is that you do not go to these things to define you. So for the Christian, being in the corner office or the mail room, being single or married, having children or not, having a car or a private plane does not matter. That is the difference. If you get up in the morning and say, "I will feel good about myself if ____ happens," then you are not embracing the Gospel.

The Gospel says that God feels good about us because of what Jesus has done. We feel good about ourselves because of what Jesus has done, not because we are good and are beautiful snowflakes deserving the love of everyone. Rather, we should say, "I rise and fall, but what I have put my hope in does not."

Finally, to find hope in the Gospel is to know God doesn't promise a future outcome in this life. In Genesis 12, Abram is told by God to go and leave everything behind, but he is not told anything of what is to come. All Abram knows is that God has made a promise and that he is to leave everything behind. Abram does not know how everything will work out. His only hope is that God will come through on his promise. All Abram knows is that he, his family, and the tower of Babel are not worth his hope.

Today, we can look back to the fulfilled promise of God in Jesus. We can say, "It is enough for us to know that God has promised and delivered Jesus. I do not have to know much else." The way you know you are beginning to understand the Gospel is when you are saying to God, "I believe and I will go. I am going not to earn but rather because it has been earned for me."

Chapter 9

Seeing the Call of God

Genesis 11:27–12:9

Abram means "father." Abraham means "father of many." All the major monotheistic religions—Judaism, Islam, and Christianity—agree that Abram heard from God. We disagree on almost all the answers to every big question, we have fundamental disagreements, and yet we all agree that Abram heard from God. This is significant to us because above all else, we want to hear from God. There are people saying, "I want to hear from God"; there are people saying, "I think I have heard from God, but I am not sure"; and then there are those who are saying, "I want to be reminded of the call that I have heard from God." For all of those people, the Bible says to look to Abram. Abram heard from God. Genesis 12:1 says, "Now the LORD said to Abram … " None of the major monotheistic religions dispute that the Lord, the God of the universe, spoke to Abram. When we look at the call of Abram, we want to think about what we do not see, what we do see, and what we need to see. Here, we will uncover what it means to hear from God.

What We Do Not See

First, I want to look at what we do not see in God's call to Abram. We expect, if God is interested in speaking to someone and if God has this epic plan to unveil, he is going to look for the best and the brightest person. That is not what we see here, but that is how we relate to God. We think this way because this is what we do. When we are looking to be in relationship, we look for the best and the brightest. We don't walk into a room to the guy who is slobbering and picking his nose and say, "Would you like to be my friend?" Instead, we think, *You are like the people you spend time with, so choose wisely.* We walk into a room and evaluate people based on what they can do for us. We are looking for the best and the brightest, so we assume that God is looking for the best and the brightest. We think that God is interested in speaking to people who earn it. We think God is looking for people who are very moral, good, honest, and full of integrity because if we were God, that is what we would look for.

Abram is not that guy. When you read the text, you see that if God were surveying the earth, if he were looking for the best and the brightest, he would not pick Abram. First, Abram is an idol worshiper. We see in chapter 11 that his father's name is Terah, which is derived from the name of an old moon god. We see that Abram lives in Ur of the Chaldeans. It is a place noted in history for worshipping the moon god.

Also, physically speaking, Abram is not the best choice. We see in the text that he is seventy-five years old and his wife is sterile. We are going to see that God's plan for Abram is, through Abram, to birth a nation. In order to do that, Abram has to have children. Abram is old and his wife is barren. Physically, he does not fit the bill.

Finally, on a personality level, Abram does not fit. If you read ahead in the story of Abram, you will find that he is a coward. On multiple occasions when going to a foreign country, his wife (who apparently was attractive in her old age) is taken by foreign dictators for their own pleasure. They never sleep with her because God intervenes miraculously, but Abram is going to let them. He is a coward.

Not only is he a coward, but he is a homebody. We see in chapter 11 that Abram lives where his dad lived and died. He is not looking to travel. This is not Odysseus in *The Odyssey*, heading out on a great journey.

Abram in no way is the guy anybody would consider the best and the brightest. He is old, his wife is barren, he is a moon-worshiper, and he is a coward. This is not who God would call if God's call were earned.

The other heroes of the Bible were not paragons of virtue, either. Moses splits the Red Sea. Moses goes to Pharaoh. Moses is a big, famous guy, yet when God's call came to him in a burning bush, Moses was a fugitive on the run for committing murder.

How about David? We all remember David and Goliath, mighty King David, the one who sets Israel on a trajectory to thrive as a kingdom. Yet when God's call came to David, he was the runt of the litter. He was the kid his dad did not even think to call.

Even the entire nation of Israel was not chosen because it earned the call. Listen to what God says to Israel in Deuteronomy 7:7: "It was not because you were more in number than any other people that the LORD set his love on you and chose you, for you were the fewest of all peoples."

This tells us two things about the call of God. First, it always comes in grace. No one has ever earned the call of God. God is not searching the earth for the best and the brightest, because there are no best and brightest. The reality is that all of us at our cores are moon worshipers. We are all at our cores physically broken, cowards, or homebodies. If you look at us hard enough, there is something there to disqualify us. God is not looking for those who earn the call; he is looking to give it graciously. Many of us implore God and say, "God, speak to me!" and we think he is obligated to answer because we showed up. In our hearts, we are hoping that if we pray enough and with enough passion, God is going to have to speak to us. We open the Bible and we believe God is obligated to speak to us, but God's call has never been based on human merit, human effort, or obligation. If Abram, who went on to become Abraham, who is revered by three monotheistic religions, could not earn the call of God, why would you and I think we could? God's call comes only in grace.

Second, God's call is God-centered. If God does not speak to people on the basis of merit, then it must be because God desires to do something great in people who are incapable of greatness on their own. God speaks to Abram not because Abram deserves it but precisely because he does not. When Abram becomes Abraham and does all these great things, you can't say, "I always knew he had it in him!" because he did not. He had it in him because God spoke to him and because God's call is gracious.

Today, we know Abraham not because he earned the call of God but because he received it—not because he achieved it but because he received it. We cannot expect to earn God's call. It does not matter how many times you pray or how many times you read the Bible; you cannot earn God's call. God's call comes in grace. We never see God looking for someone who has earned it.

What We Do See

If you think you can earn the call of God and you say something like, "If I am good enough, God has to speak to me," then when God speaks to you, you will expect it to be a word of affirmation. If you have to earn God's favor, then when he speaks, he is going to say, "Good job." Yet in God's call to Abram, there is no affirmation language. If you go to most churches nowadays, what you hear preached are messages of affirmation: "God loves you for you. God sees potential in you. God has great plans for you. God is so excited you have come, so he can bask in the glow of you." That is not what is going on in Genesis 12. We are not told one positive thing about Abram prior to God speaking to him.

You cannot have both grace and affirmation. You cannot have your relationship with God be based primarily on grace and expect an affirmation. The essence of grace is "I do not deserve it, but I am going to get it." God shows up to Abram and says, "You do not deserve it, but I am going to do something in you. And because you do not deserve it, I am going to change you." God's call is not one of affirmation but one of transformation. God's call is not preoccupied with telling you how wonderful you are and how you are a snowflake and there is no one else like you.

Look at what happens to Abram. God graciously calls and says, "Leave your country and go to a different land." Abram replies, "Okay." God speaks to him in grace, Abram responds in simple faith, and God uses that faith to change Abram. There are three ways God changes Abram. First, Abram leaves the known for the unknown. Genesis 12:1 says, "Now the LORD said to Abram, 'Go from your country and your kindred and your father's house to the land I will show you.'" God tells Abram to leave everything he is familiar with and go to a land he has never traveled. There is no interstate and he has no cell phone. He is never going to see his family again. God's call comes to Abram and says, "Though you do not deserve it, I have a plan for you," and the plan says, "You have to move. You have to be transformed. You have to leave the familiar for the unfamiliar." Abram is seventy-five; he is not looking to leave home. He is settled, and yet God's call comes and says, "I am going to move you from the known to the unknown."

God also says, "I have a plan for you, but it involves leaving your own efforts for my efforts." Look at Genesis 12:2: "And I will make of you a great nation. And I will bless you and make your name great so you will be a blessing." Who is not going to move if God says that? God is really saying to Abram, "You have been trying to make your name great in Ur of the Chaldeans, but I want you to completely abandon your own efforts. I have my own efforts, my own plan, and my own promise." God is telling Abram to leave the seen for the unseen.

Genesis 12:7 says, "At that time, the Canaanites were in the land. Then the LORD appeared to Abram and said, 'to your offspring I will give this land.' So he built there an altar to the LORD who had appeared to him … and Abram journeyed on." Abram is walking, but he does not even know where. He gets to Canaan, and God says, "Look around," but he does not say, "This is going to be yours." Rather, he says, "This is going to be your descendants'. It is going to be your children's. It is going to be future generations'." God is telling Abram to keep moving.

God's call came to Abram in grace, and it completely transformed Abram. This is not out of the norm. God comes to Moses, a fugitive on the run for committing murder, and after God's visit, Moses goes back to the place where he is a fugitive, faces down the world leader, and leads God's people. David goes from runt of the litter to mighty King David. Israel goes from the least of all the nations to flourish under David and Solomon. God's call comes in grace, but it always changes the people to whom it comes.

Through simple faith, Abraham says, "I am going," when God says, "Go." In his going, God changes him. This is the mark of hearing the call of God. You may want to know "Have I heard the call of God?" You have heard the call of God when God reveals your inadequacy and transforms you through simple faith. Abram hears the call of God and is transformed.

Why does God change him from Abram to Abraham? Because God transforms him; because God's call wrecks his life and gives him a new life instead. A proof of having heard the call of God is being transformed by grace.

What We Need to See

We do not see God saying, "Who deserves it?" We see God's call come to Abram and wreck him, then build him up and change him at his very core. What do we need to see? For many of us, we think if there is a God and he wants to be in relationship with us, he should give us some evidence. The God of the Bible does not completely disagree with that. In fact, he calls Abram to do something. He says to Abram, "Go and leave your country. I am going to do this great thing." Abram gets to Canaan, and God says, "Keep moving." All along, Abram knows there is one piece of evidence that has to be there if he is going to know that the God who made this promise to him is trustworthy: Abram has to have a son. The promise of God means nothing without a son. Abram travels on, but he has to be thinking, *If this is going to happen, I have to have a son. I cannot be made the father of a great nation if I do not have a son to whom I can pass on a nation.* If he has a daughter, the daughter is going to live with her husband and be a part of the nation that her husband is building, not part of God's chosen nation promised to Abram. Abram has to have a son. So Abram moves forward without a physical sign, but eventually, he is going to get one.

When Abram finally gets to look at Isaac, his first thought is not, *I love you, Isaac; you are so wonderful.* That would be his second thought. Every time he looks at Isaac, every time he messes up Isaac's hair, every time they wrestle, every time they do whatever fathers and sons do, Abram is going to say, "This is the proof that God is keeping his promise." Every time Abram looks at Isaac, it is still the look of faith. All he has is Isaac. Isaac is not a nation. Isaac is just a son. Trusting God's promise is still an act of faith for Abram, but he has faith in the evidence that God has provided him through Isaac.

We are prone to thinking, *If only I had what Abram had, I could be a person of faith,* yet the God of the Bible makes the same call to everyone that he makes to Abram. God calls Abram and says, "Believe in my promises, and as evidence of these promises, I give you a son." When Abram looks at Isaac, he knows the promises of God are going to come to fruition through him. Isaac has a son, Jacob, then Isaac dies. It takes a long time for the promises to come to fruition. Isaac was not the promise keeper; he was a sign of the promise. Jacob is not the promise keeper. He is not even that good of a guy. He has many sons, and then he dies. Jacob was not the promise keeper; he was a son of a promise. Abraham's progeny keep having sons, and the descendants of Abraham grow and grow. Each son is a sign of the promise, but they are not in and of themselves promise keepers, until we get to Matthew 1. Matthew says the promise goes from Abraham to David to a guy named Joseph in Bethlehem. To him a son is born, Jesus Christ. It is in Jesus that the promises to Abraham are realized.

We may think, *The promise was the nation of Israel.* The problem with this thinking is that God says to Abraham, "I am going to make you into a nation, and your nation is going to bless all the nations of the earth." But if you read the Old Testament, you will read that Israel does not do that. They are at war with many of the nations. At their best, they are isolationists who build big walls and hope not to be stained by the world. Jesus, right before he leaves for the cross, says to his followers, "Go, therefore, into all the nations" (Acts 1:8). Why does Jesus say this? Because he is the fulfillment of the promise to Abraham. When Jesus goes to the cross, the promise is fulfilled. By dying for the sins of the church and rising from the dead, Jesus becomes a blessing to people from all nations. He is building a new nation, the nation of Abraham. Jesus shows up as the promise keeper of Abraham. Jesus says to us, "I have come in grace. You did not earn me." He comes in grace and says through faith that he will transform people just like God transformed Abraham.

God said to Abraham, "Trust me. To show you can trust me, I am sending a son." God says to people today, "Trust me. To show you can trust me, I have sent a son—Jesus." When Abram looks at Isaac, he is not seeing Isaac; he is seeing Isaac's son. He is seeing a nation. He is seeing a group of people, and he knows that in order for his nation to be a blessing to all the nations, something big has to happen. When he looks at Isaac, he is seeing, without even knowing it, generations ahead, to Jesus.

Abram leaves his country in anticipation of Jesus. Thousands of years before Jesus will be born, Abram is looking ahead to Jesus. God says to us, "You look back to Jesus like Abraham looked forward to Jesus, because I have sent a son." The call comes in grace, and it transforms us. The evidence of that is in the son. So Jesus goes to the cross and says, "It is finished" (John 19:30). Here, he is saying, "I have come in grace and done what you cannot do. I have died for the sins that you could not have paid for. I have reconciled you to God in a way that you could not." When he rises from the dead and ascends to heaven, what happens to everyone who knows him? They are changed. There is Peter, who is a coward like Abram, but then he meets Jesus. Jesus rises from the dead, Peter sees this, and the next thing you know he is preaching to thousands of people the good news of the Gospel. Why? Because, like Abraham, he receives the call of God in grace through Jesus and is utterly transformed.

Everyone agrees that Abram heard from God. Only Christianity comes full circle and says not only did God make the promises to Abraham but kept the promises through Jesus. Why does Matthew's gospel start with a genealogy? Matthew is saying, "Remember, God made promises to Abram? He kept them through the Son. That son was not Isaac. He was a marker, but the greater Son was Jesus Christ."

If you are not a Christian, you can pray until you are blue in the face, but because you have sinned against God, your prayers never go further than the ceiling. You are never going to pray enough for God to speak with you. We do not merit the call of God. That call comes to us in grace. It came to Abraham that way, it came to Moses that way, it came to David that way, and it came to Israel that way. Do we really think that Moses could not earn it but we can?

How do I know that God has spoken to me? How do I know he is going to change me? How do I know he is going to keep his promises? The same way Abraham did: We look at the Son. We do not have to hear the call of God anymore, but rather we see it in Christ. From now on, no one has to listen for God anymore; we can look at Jesus on the cross. That is the call of God. Our call today is through simple faith when we believe he died for our sin and rose from the dead, making atonement between us and God, reconciling God and us. It is through Jesus that we are transformed. Abram did not get off the couch until God spoke. Today, God is not looking for us to get off the couch until we listen to what he has said through Jesus. The call of God is not about earning, it is about being transformed. The call of God is not about achieving, it is about receiving.

If you are a Christian and you believe these things but are struggling with doubt or insecurity, you need to look to Jesus. Where do you think Abraham went if times got tough? Where do you think he went when it felt like God might not keep his promise? Where do you think he went when he could not see the promise? He cuddled with Isaac. He went for a walk with Isaac. He looked at Isaac. People struggle today and they say, "I need to read my Bible. I need to pray more." Yes, we do need to do those things, but in doing them, we always need to look to Jesus. Why does the Bible have value? In it we find Jesus, the Son, the one through whom God has shown us he keeps his promises. Why do we need to pray? We need to pray to cling to Jesus. When Abraham went for a walk with Isaac, it was not in the walk that he found comfort; it was with whom he was walking. It is not in the praying or the reading or the doing or the going that we will find comfort. It is in the one to whom we are praying to, reading to, doing for, or going to that we will find comfort.

Are you envious of Abraham? Sometimes I am. But Abraham would have traded places with you in a second. All he had was a little boy. He did not know how God was going to do what he was going to do. We have a crucified Son of God.

The book of Hebrews goes through the heroes of the faith, but in the end, the author says these people only have a promise (Hebrews 11). We have so much more. Then the author of Hebrews writes, "Therefore, since we are surrounded by so great a cloud of witnesses, let us also lay aside every weight and sin which clings so closely ... looking to Jesus" (Hebrews 12:1–2a). Moses would have traded his burning bush for your knowledge of Jesus in a second. David would have traded his anointing to know the Son, because what we have is greater. Do not be envious of Abram. Abram had a little boy; we have the body and blood of Jesus. God said to Abram, "Go and I will give you a son," but to us, he says, "I have given you a son; now go."

If you are not a Christian, there is nothing more asked of you than to consider the call of Jesus. He came in grace because you did not deserve it. You will never deserve it. You have to lay that thought down and come to Jesus saying, "I could not earn it. You have done for me what I could not do. Because I know the Son, you will change me and you should change me because I need to be changed." We are rescued not by the changing but by the grace. If you are a Christian, do what Abram did and look to the Son. It is only there you are going to find comfort. It is only there you are going to find peace. It is only there you are going to find hope in a world that struggles with doubt.

Chapter 10

The One God Says Is Righteous

Genesis 15

"**A**nd he believed the LORD and it was counted to him as righteousness" (Genesis 15:6) is probably the most important verse in all the Old Testament. You have to understand what is happening in this verse to understand the Bible as a whole and to understand Christianity. If you understand Genesis 15:6, the Bible and Christianity start to make sense. If you do not understand Genesis 15:6, they will never make sense. In Genesis 15:6, you see that God is declaring a man to be righteous. All of the world's religions are aimed at making people righteous. They may not use that language, but religion is primarily a transactional thing, built around the idea that if you do certain things or follow certain principals, God will accept you. Religion sets a path, and we seek to travel on it. If we go down the path the right way, we are accepted. If we go down the wrong way, we are not accepted.

Here we see a man, Abram, being accepted by God. If we all come to religion saying, "If there is a God, I want him to accept me," then we have to look at Abram and say, "What did he have? What does he know? What is true about him that I need to know in order to be declared righteous by God?" To answer these questions, we have two goals. First, we need to understand this verse so that we can understand the Bible as a whole. We need to get this verse and use it as an interpretive lens through which to see the whole story of Christianity. Second, we must discover what made Abraham righteous before God so that we can understand how God can call us righteous as well.

Why It Must Be Faith

All religion is aimed at being righteous before God, and all people are driven to want this righteousness at one time or another in their lives. When we think about righteousness, we think primarily in terms of earning, meriting, or deserving. We believe that if we are good enough or devoted enough, God will be obligated to see us as righteous and worthy. We go about life trying to be very moral, trying to rise to the occasion, to take stands and be strong. We also go through life trying to be religiously devoted. We pray a lot, read the Bible a lot, and go to church services a lot. We try to do whatever it takes to be the kind of man or woman to whom God says, "Yes! You are good enough. You are righteous." This is innate in us as humans.

We live in a culture that tells us we can do whatever we want. We have this belief system in our culture that says if you want to do something and you set your mind to it and work to do it, you will accomplish it if you work hard enough, and that if you do not accomplish your goal, it is because you did not try hard enough. As children, we are told we can be anything we want to be, if we just do the work and believe in our dreams. There is an innate human drive that says that nothing in life is worthwhile unless you earn it. We then apply this belief system to God and think, *I can earn my way into being accepted by God.*

It is not obvious that we think this way; it is very subtle. Imagine that you walk outside and get hit by a bus and in an instant you are standing before God and he asks, "Why should I accept you?" You would probably respond, "Because I am a good person." Most of us would say that. But in what sense do we mean that we are good people? There is not a morality scale with which we can measure our goodness, like we are a seven out of ten. When we say, "I am a good person," what we are really saying is "I am a good enough person. I have done enough, achieved enough, and earned enough. There may be some moral action that I did not quite attain, but I did enough. There are people more devoted than me, but I was devoted enough." We expect for God to say we are good enough, because we think we are good enough.

There are probably others who do not think they are good enough. Some of us are driven by insecurity, saying we need to be good enough, but we are not really sure that we are good enough. We try to put one more thing in the "win" column and one less in the "lose" column, so in the end, we have enough in the "win" column to be accepted by God. Still others turn off religion as a whole. They say, "I am tired of wondering if I am good enough, so I have decided there is no God. Or maybe there is, but I cannot really know him, so I am just checking out."

Whether you are the person who says, "I am good enough," or the one who says, "I do not know if I am good enough," or the one who says, "I have stopped wondering if I am good enough," the reality is that all of us, when we think about righteousness, think about it in terms of earning, meriting, and deserving.

Genesis 15:6 flies in the face of that thinking. If we think we earn righteousness, Genesis 15:6 says we are absolutely, fundamentally, and categorically wrong. The word "counted" in 15:6 is also translated as "credited" and "reckoned." In other words, Moses is saying that God looks at Abram and says, "That guy has no righteousness." God sees only his simple faith, and on the basis of that faith, God credits righteousness to his account. God looks at Abram's simple faith and says, "It will do. I am going to give him righteousness." This is what Christians call grace, which is unmerited favor. Grace is God looking at Abram and saying, "You have no righteousness. You are not moral and you are not religiously devout, but I will give you what you do not deserve, what you have not earned, and what you could never earn."

Back when people used to write checks, they could not process them right away. If you wrote a check on Friday afternoon, you could float it over the weekend until Monday morning, when you hoped you would have the money in your account. It is like Abram wrote a check knowing there was not enough money in his account. A few days later, instead of hearing that his check bounced or his account was overdrawn, he found that someone came along and put money that was not his into his account. That is what is happening here. God is crediting Abram with righteousness. Abram has a zero balance, and God is putting righteousness in the account.

Why does our Abram's relationship with God have to be through faith? Because that is all Abram has. God does not say, "Abram, you have to be very moral to be righteous," because Abram is not good enough. Shortly before this verse, Abram was offering his wife out. That is the moral equivalent of failing the final exam. If God were to say, "Abram, you can only be righteous if you are religiously devout enough," Abram would fail. In Genesis 11, where we first find Abram, he was worshipping the moon. God is giving Abram grace, which he does not deserve, on the basis of Abram's simple faith. What is Abram's simple faith? He says, "The only way I can keep moving and going is if God is doing something, because I have nothing." Abram is not righteous, he has not earned righteousness, he is not good enough, and he is not devout enough, but God says to him, "You have a zero balance, but I will give you grace."

Grace is a beautiful thing, but it is not easy to grasp. In our culture of earning, grace is not an easy thing. It can cause an identity crisis. We do not handle grace well, because grace requires us to admit that we have a zero balance. In order for someone to show us grace, we have to admit that what they are giving us, we cannot earn; otherwise, what they are giving us is not grace. Our culture says, "If you want to know

God, you have to earn it. You have to work hard. God will be fair, and fair will be to your benefit." Grace says, "You can try hard; it will not matter. You can work hard; it will not matter. God will be fair, but it will not be for your benefit. You have a zero balance." In Genesis 15:6, we see that Abram has only simple faith, and it is credited to him as righteousness. He does not have moral fortitude, moral certainty, or religious devotion. That means the righteousness of God cannot be earned.

What This Does Not Mean

In order for us to understand Christianity, the first step we take must be to see that we have a zero balance morally, religiously, and spiritually. Earning righteousness, earning a standing before God, does not fit in this passage. Abram does not deserve it, but he gets it. Our culture tells us we can accomplish anything to which we set our minds, but God says there is one thing we are never going to get by setting our minds on it. Grace is a wonderful thing, but we are never going to get it unless we believe, like Abram, that we have a zero balance. Are we willing to go there? Are we willing to say we have a zero balance? Are we willing to say that at our cores, we are morally bankrupt and our only hope is that God gives righteousness not on the basis of earning it? Righteousness must be given through faith, because that is all we can bring to the table.

Our desire to earn righteousness is so insidious that even when we talk about it being through faith, we still find a way to turn faith into earning. We see Abram had simple faith and God credited it to him as righteousness, so we say to ourselves, "That means I need to have faith like Abram!" We read Genesis 15:6 as "And he believed the LORD with a special, super kind of faith, and when the LORD saw that special, super kind of faith, he had no choice but to declare him righteous!" When we think about faith, we think it must have been a faith that was strong and certain. We think it must be the kind of faith that says no matter what happens to us or around us, we put our heads down and say, "I believe," until we power through any obstacle. We believe it has to be an unrelenting, unquestioning, driving faith. No matter what God says to do, we are going to do it, because super faith gets us to righteousness. Except when we read the Bible, we discover Abram does not have super-strong faith. In Genesis 15:1, God repeats his promise to Abram and Abram asks the Lord for more proof. He says to God, "I have heard your promise, but it has been years and years and I still do not have a child. I believe you, but I do not believe you. I have belief, but I also have unbelief." Abram has weak faith; he is not powering through. He is saying, "When is this going to happen?" In many ways, it is harder to live with a promise that has not happened yet than it is to live without a promise.

Well, if it is not super-strong faith, then it must be super-certain faith, we then think—except Abram does not have that kind of faith, either. Immediately after God credits righteousness to Abram, Abram says, "Oh LORD God, how am I to know I shall possess it?" (Genesis 15:7). He is telling God that he has doubts. Abram does not have a strong or certain faith; he has a simple, doubting, questioning, weak faith, yet God declares him righteous.

Abram's faith was not primarily volitional; it was not first an act of the will. It was also not primarily intellectual. His faith was primarily relational. Abram did not believe in God; he believed God. He did not believe in God as a kind of intellectual proposition; he believed God personally and relationally. At the end of this chapter, God does not rebuke Abram for coming to him with more doubt; instead, he tells Abram to get some animals. Abram cuts the animals in half and lays them out. This is contractual language and action. In Abram's day, if you wanted to make something binding, you cut animals in half and both parties would walk through the carcasses. The parties were saying, "If I do not uphold my end of the contract, may it be done to me as it has been done to these animals." But this scene is not of Abram making a contract he has to uphold. Abram thinks that is happening, but while he is waiting for God to show up for the contractual ceremony, he falls asleep. While Abram is sleeping, God says, "Know for certain [these things are going to happen]" (Genesis 15:13a), and to prove it, God himself walks through the animals in the metaphorical image of the pot and the fire (Genesis 15:17). God is saying to Abram, "Do not believe in your own moral ability, religious devotion, or super-strong faith. Believe in me. If what I promise does not happen, I will be cut in half." He does not ask Abram to walk through the animals, because none of the promises depends on Abram. God says, "Abram, do not believe in a promise. Believe in me. I am putting myself on the line, and I am putting my name on the line. I am walking through."

What This Does Mean

This means the kind of faith that makes you righteous is the kind of faith that says, "I have a zero balance, but I believe in God's grace. God has orchestrated the world in such a way that he walks through the animals and keeps the promises I break." Every other religion would say we walk through the animals with God. Only the Bible says the only thing we bring to the equation is our snoring. That is all Abram does while God walks through. Our only hope is that God is doing something, because we are incapable of doing that very same thing.

Today, we can think, *If God gave me a sign like he gave Abram, I would have simple faith like Abram.* But God has given us that sign. Moses writes, "As the sun was going down, a deep sleep fell on Abram. And behold, dreadful and great darkness fell upon him" (Genesis 15:12). This verse foreshadows Christ on the cross. When Christ is dying on the cross, the sky goes dreadfully dark because in that moment, God is passing through the discarded animals. God is being torn in two on the cross not because he did not keep his part of the promise but because we did not keep our part. As the sky goes dark, God is saying, "You have not lived up to my expectations. You are not good enough. You will never be good enough. You can set your mind to it all you want, but you will never be good enough. I am taking your place. I will be ripped in two for your sin in order that you might believe." In that moment, Christ is dying for our negative balance and we are being credited with his righteousness. God is doing something for me that I cannot do for myself. Our simple faith is to believe in that moment.

All other monotheistic religions believe Abram heard from God, but they miss the point. Abram was not a religious superman. His hope was in the God who put himself on the line to see his promise come to fruition. It is the same for us. Our hope is not in our religious devotion or moral fortitude. Our hope is in a God who put himself on the line, dying for our sin and rising from the dead so we may simply look at the cross and say, "My hope is in the God who was ripped in two when it should have been me." Jesus says, "This is my body and my blood broken and shed for you" (Luke 22:19–20), because our bodies and our blood should have been broken, but his were instead.

If you want to understand Christianity, you have to see yourself as someone like Abram. Abram did not have righteousness apart from the credit deposited to him from God. It has to be that way for us. Christianity has grace, but deep in our souls, we do not love grace because grace comes to us and says we have nothing. We think we have something, but anything we have does not measure up, so it is as good as nothing. Our only hope is that Christ had everything, and he gave it in our place. Our hope is the same hope of Abram: a simple faith in the God who says, "All you bring to the table is snoring, but I will walk through for you."

If you are a Christian and you say, "I do not feel close to God, and I have not felt close to God for some time," you will be tempted to run to a lie that says, "If I do not feel close to God, it is because I have stopped doing, and I need to start doing." You are going to read your Bible and you are going to pray, but you never got to God on the basis of your own actions in the first place. You did not begin with God that way, and you will not sustain your life with God that way. Your only hope is to come to God and say, "All that I have is like snoring. My only hope is that Christ had everything, and he gave it all for me. My only hope is that though I am completely deficient, he is completely sufficient. And somehow, in his grace, my deficiency got swallowed up by his sufficiency."

You can read the Bible until you are blue in the face, but you are not going to get any closer to God. The Bible is a means to an end. It is the means through which you understand that you are deficient and he is sufficient. If you are not going to the Bible to get that, the Bible will never help you. If you are not praying to get that, the Bible will never help you. If you are not close to God, it is not because you have not been doing; it is because you have forgotten that you are completely and utterly deficient but he is completely and utterly sufficient.

If you are not a Christian, every other world religion, and even a lot of churches with crosses on their signs, will tell you if you want to be close to God, you have to do, because that resonates with you. The Gospel says, "In all your doing, you have not yet found God. You have a zero balance, and your only hope is not that God will lay the animals out and you will power through them. Your only hope is that God walked through them. Do not try to be religiously devoted and think God will accept you. Do not try to be morally good and think God will accept you. Rather, look to the one who is perfectly religiously devoted and perfectly morally good, who went to the cross for the church." Those who respond to Christ in simple faith, those who can sing, "Nothing in my hands I bring, simply to the cross I cling," will be declared righteous by God. Abraham was clinging to a smoking pot; we cling to a savior on the cross. We take up communion, our symbol of the body and the blood, and we say, "I used to have a zero balance, but now I have an infinite balance because of this body and this blood, because of this man broken for me."

Chapter 11

The God Who Promises and Provides

Genesis 17

G od shows up immediately in Genesis 17. Moses writes, "When Abram was ninety-nine years old the Lord appeared to Abram" (Genesis 17:1a). This passage is a marker that gives us context so we understand that approximately thirteen years have passed since Abram slept with Hagar and had Ishmael. Abram made a colossal mistake. It is going to have massive implications not just for his family but also the world, and thirteen years after this mistake, God shows up. Listen to what God says to Abram: "I am God Almighty. Walk before me, and be blameless" (Genesis 17:1b). In these three phrases, we can see exactly what God is saying to Abram and what he wants from us.

The first thing God says is "I am God Almighty." God is telling Abram that he wants to be seen for who he really is. In the Hebrew, the name is "El Shaddai," the God whose purposes cannot be thwarted, or the

God who is invincible. He is invincible in the sense that whatever he purposes to do is going to be done. God is saying to Abram, "I am the one who sets my plan, and nobody messes with it. I am the one who cannot be opposed. I am the one who is bigger and stronger than everybody."

This is so different from our Western culture's view of God. Who has not been to a Bible study, coffee-table conversation, or a bar-table conversation where someone is saying, "I think God is like this ... " or "To me, God is like this ... "? God is saying to Abram, and saying implicitly to us, "You need to know when you talk with me and when you engage me, I am God Almighty. I am bigger than you. I am stronger than you. My purposes are greater than yours. I am going to do what I set out to do. I am in every way bigger, better, and stronger than you."

In Western culture, we want to make God into our own image. We want to pontificate and elaborate, but God requires that we see him for who he really is. God is very passionate about making sure that Abraham knows the answer to the question "Who is God?" God is saying to Abram, "When someone asks you that question or when you ask yourself that question, here is what you say: 'El Shaddai. God is strong. God is powerful. God's purposes cannot be thwarted.'" There is no coincidence here that God is using that name in connection with the guy who thought he would circumvent God's plans himself. God is saying to Abram, "No, my plans remain."

Next, God says, "Walk before me." This expression means, "Because of who I am, understand that what I think, what I want, and what I say is best matters." When he says, "Walk before me," he is saying, "Abram, because of who I am, to know me should mean that you seek to live in such a way that pleases me and that shows you believe I am the one who knows best." He is not saying this accidentally. Thirteen years ago, God said to Abram, "You are going to have a son." Then Sarah came to Abraham and said, "You know, I am not going to have a son, but maybe we kind of could if we took my slave and got her pregnant." In that instance, Abram was not walking before God; he was walking before Sarah. He was listening to her, he was doing what she thought was best, and he was being influenced by her. Here, God is saying, "Not only do I want you to know who I am, I want to be the key influencer in your life. I want you to do things the way I say to do them. I want you to think about things the way I say to think about them. I want to be seen for who I am, and I want to be responded to accordingly." Finally, he says, "And be blameless." This word, "blameless," here does not just mean moral effort. It means a kind of sincerity that is both internal and external. It is not doing the right thing with insincere hearts. When God says, "And be blameless," he is saying to Abraham, "I want to be seen for who I am. I want you to respond accordingly, and I want you to do it with absolute sincerity. I do not want you to just do the right thing; I want you to want the right thing. I want you to believe it is the right thing. I do not want you to just obey me, Abram; I want you to obey me with a sincere heart. I want what drives you to obey to be both internal and external."

That is what God wants from people, and we want the same thing. When we are in relationship with somebody, we want them to see us for who we really are; we want them to respond to us accordingly, and we want them to be sincere.

God is more than a person, but he is not less than a person. If we want to be seen for who we are, if we want to be responded to for who we are, and if we want people to respond to us with sincerity, so does God. What the Bible is really saying about sin is this: Sin is not checking the wrong boxes off and missing the right ones. Instead, sin is failing to do one of the following: to see God for who he really is, to respond accordingly, or to respond to him with sincerity.

Ultimately, to sin is to depersonalize God. Sin is to relate to God in a way other than the way he has asked you to relate to him. Don't you hate it when people do this to you? God does not like it when we do it to him. To strip someone of who they are is a violent thing. To strip people of their personalities, of their uniqueness, and to love them or respond to them as though they are not unique people is an act of violence. You do not like it, and God does not either.

The punishment that God inflicts upon sinners is not because God has been tallying scores. Rather, God's judgment is reserved for those who have spent their lives not seeing him for who he is, for not responding accordingly, or, if they understand those things, for responding without sincerity. In the Bible, hell is a place that exists for those who have spent their lives depersonalizing God. When you think about hell that way, hell is not nearly as difficult to understand as when we are just going around thinking about checking the right boxes.

Look at what God says next: " … that I may make my covenant between me and you and multiply you greatly" (Genesis 17:3)—in other words, "Abram, we are going to get this covenant ball rolling, but if it is really going to reach fruition, you are going to have to become someone who knows exactly who I am, who responds accordingly, and who does it with absolute sincerity."

When you ask, "What does God want from me?" you are asking a question that is the essence of all religion. It is the reason we come; it is the reason we listen; it is the reason we think. This is what he wants from you: to know who he is, to respond accordingly, and to do so with absolute sincerity.

Where We Won't Find What God Wants From Us

When we think about what God wants from us, our first response is to say, "Okay, if that is what God wants, I can do that! I can work hard and get there." The other response is to throw our hands up in despair and say, "I can never be that kind of person." These are the response of pride and the response of self-loathing.

If you respond in pride and you want to become the kind of person that can please God, you cannot look inwardly for that answer. You cannot say, "If God wants me to see him for who he is, to respond accordingly, and to do it with sincerity, then fine, I will start doing that. I will work hard. I will do my best. I will leave Post-it notes all over the house." There is one big problem: You are never going to please God by doing these things. Moreover, is that Abram's response? Is Abram a guy who knows God for who he really is and responds accordingly with sincerity? Absolutely not. You know that is not who Abram is, because God shows up and says, "Abram, this is who I am. This is what I want you to do." God does not show up and say, "Abram, keep doing what you are doing. You are doing great." Abram is not that guy.

We think we can change. It looks like Abram does, doesn't it? Abram falls on his face before God, and he says, "You are God; I am not God." It looks like Abram is changing. It looks like he gets it. It looks like he is going to move forward. It looks like all of us prideful people have hope: "If Abram can change, then I can change." The problem is, Abram does not change. In fact, he gets on his face not once but twice. At the end of the chapter, he is on his face again, only this time, he is laughing. God has just said he is going to give Abram a son through Sarah, which God already promised. God is reiterating his promise, and Abram is on his face again, but he is not worshiping; he is laughing at how ludicrous God's promise is. Then Abram lifts Ishmael up metaphorically and says, "Oh yes, God, that Ishmael might live before you."

Abram has not changed. Abram's name has changed, but he has not changed. He is laughing and offering Ishmael. Abram cannot even see that he is being crazy. He thinks he is legitimately giving God something that God might actually want. This is what we all do with God. We all offer up Ishmael. We do not admit is the tainting on all of what we do are the things we have done, or the insincere way in which we do them. We fail to see the inadequacy of the things we offer up to God.

Even the best we have to give God, our best good deeds, is Ishmael—not our illegitimate children, per se, but rather our illegitimate righteousness. This is what Isaiah means when he says, "All of us have become unclean, and all of our righteous deeds are like filthy garments" (Isaiah 64:6). Isaiah is saying that even in our best, there is a stain. The stain is insincerity, not responding to God according to his righteousness. The stain is in not seeing him as God but creating our own version of God and following that version. Abram cannot make himself the kind of person God wants him to be. God tells him, "Walk before me and be blameless," but Abram has not done that. He is not going to do that, and he is not capable of doing that. If Abram were being honest, rather than offering up Ishmael, he would be on his face, not laughing about having a child but laughing at the thought that he could ever be someone who could walk before God and be blameless. You are never going to understand Christianity until you come to see that the best you have to offer God is just like Abram offering Ishmael. The best you have to offer God is illegitimate righteousness: good actions tainted with insincerity, or good actions tainted with improper motivation. There is a preacher who says, "The best of men are men at best." The best of people are people at best. We are all tainted; we are all stained.

In verse 3, Abram is on his face and he looks good. He gets it. There will be a time in your life when you look good, sound good, and feel good, but the next time you are on your face, you will be laughing and offering up Ishmael, just like Abraham. Even if you could become a righteous person, what would become of all the times that you were not righteous?. Even if Abram, from that day forward, said, "I will be better," would it really erase what he had done to Hagar? Would it really erase what he had done to Sarah? It would not. It could not.

Where We Will Find What God Wants From Us

If we are not going to be who God wants us to be by looking in the mirror of self-effort, then we are left with self-loathing. This passage is great because even though Abram is on his face, laughing and offering up Ishmael, God still promises him things. When you read God's words in verse 3, " ...that I may keep my covenant... " you can read it as conditional: If Abram does not become that kind of guy, if Abram does not get busy about becoming that guy, he is not going to get anything. But that is not what happens. God makes his promise, and then he keeps going. He says, "No longer shall you be called Abram, you shall be called Abraham, for I have made you the father of a multitude of nations" (Genesis 17:5). God does not say to Abraham, "Walk before me and be blameless. I will wait. I am God, I am not in a hurry. You go ahead. Give me at least a month of good behavior, and I will get back to you." He says, "Walk before me and be blameless." He then changes Abram's name before Abraham walks before him and is blameless, not afterwards. He says, "I am going to give you children. I am going to multiply you. I am going to make you great. I am going to do all these things." If Abram had to walk before God and be blameless and yet had not as of yet, what is going on here when God blesses him anyway? The only thing God requires of Abraham is circumcision. All he requires from Abraham is a sign (Genesis 17:10–14).

God is saying to Abraham and to the men in his family, "You are going to get bloody. You are going to give up a little bit of yourself as a sign that your trust should not be in your faithfulness but rather in mine." God does not say, "Here is the deal: You have to walk before me and be blameless or you have to be circumcised." Rather, God is saying, "Here is what I want you to be. You are not that. But I am going to bless you. This sign will show you that you are not who I want you to be but I am going to bless you anyway. It will be a sign that you belong to me and you are trusting in me."

The sign means that God is not looking for Abram to become Abraham on his own. Rather, he is looking for someone else to get Abram to Abraham. How can God bless a man who is not what he said that man should be? The only way he can do that is if he knows another man is going to be that man. The only way he can do that is if he knows Abram has no chance on his own, that Abram's only chance is in someone else. Who is that someone else? Jesus.

God says to Abraham, "Kings shall come from you" (Genesis 17:6c). What is God referencing? Jesus Christ. In the genealogy in Matthew 1, we travel from Abraham to King David fourteen generations later. Then from David and the line of kings, we finally get to Jesus. Jesus is the King born from the genealogy of Abraham. Jesus is El Shaddai, the God whose plans cannot be thwarted. He becomes Emmanuel, God with us. In Genesis 17, God comes near to Abram and does not destroy Abram but rather makes promises to Abram—promises that include overcoming who Abram is. Jesus is the same way. He is God with us, but he is also God near to us. He is God whose plans cannot be thwarted. We see Jesus healing and casting out demons. He is the powerful God, but he is also God made near.

What did Jesus talk about while on earth? Sincerity. Remember what Jesus says in the Sermon on the Mount? He says, "You have heard that it was said, 'You shall not commit adultery. But I say to you that everyone who looks at a woman with lustful intent has already committed adultery with her in his heart" (Matthew 5:28). He is saying, "You cannot just walk before God and do the right thing; you have to want the right thing. You have to be completely and utterly sincere." God is looking to Abraham and saying, "Here is who I want you to be, Abraham. You are not that, but I am going to make you promises anyway." God knows that he is the promise maker and is also going to be the promise keeper in Jesus. Jesus is the only man who ever lived every minute of every day knowing who God was, responding accordingly and with absolute sincerity. He is the only one who has ever done that. When we look at Jesus, we see exactly what it means to know God, to respond to him, to love him, and to do these things with absolute sincerity.

No longer is circumcision the way to identify God as promise keeper in the church; it has been replaced by baptism. Baptism is the new circumcision (Colossians 2:11–12). Baptism is the outward sign that says you stand with God. Circumcision was bloody. Baptism is bloodless. In circumcision, Abraham is saying, "It is not in me I am trusting, but in

God. I am shedding myself to show that I am trusting God." In baptism, we are saying, "It is not the shedding of our blood in which we trust, but rather in the shedding of the blood of Christ." Circumcision had people shed their own blood as a sign they stood with God. Baptism points to the one whose blood was shed in order that we might stand with God.

The Gospel is the only message that appeals to both the prideful person and the self-loathing person. To the prideful person, it says, "You are never going to get there. You can try all you want, but someone has gotten there in your place, and He can make you what you are trying to become." The Gospel says to the prideful person, "What you want to be accomplished will be accomplished, but not in your strength. It will be accomplished in the strength of Jesus." To the self-loathing person, the Gospel says, "You are absolutely right. You are never going to be whom God wants you to be, yet God became that perfect person in your place through Jesus." Jesus is the only one who has ever responded to God perfectly all the time, and yet on the cross, when he is being crucified, he takes the place of all of us who have responded to God with absolute insincerity. He takes that punishment, and then, rising from the dead, he says, "Those who come to me on the basis of simple grace through simple faith can see their sin put on me, and my righteousness, my always knowing who God is, always responding to him accordingly, and always doing it with sincerity, goes to them." When God sees Jesus on the cross, he sees our sin, but when God sees those who believe, he sees Christ's righteousness.

Abram's hope was not in himself. He could not look inwardly but rather had to look to the same God who was making a promise. The Gospel is the only worldview that says, "Yes, God wants you to be this, but because he knows you are never going to get there, he was that in your place. Through Jesus, he is making you into that."

If you are not a Christian, the challenge for you from Genesis 17 is that you are not who God wants you to be. None of us are. You do not know who God is, you do not respond accordingly, and you do not respond with sincerity—and yet God is still fully willing and fully capable to make promises to you through Jesus, just like he did to Abraham. But unlike Abraham, you do not have to get bloody, because one has gotten bloody in your place; rather, you simply identify with his death and resurrection.

If you are a Christian, you must understand that Abram could not say, "I have to go be. I have to go do." So many Christians get into such a low place, their relationship with the Lord is not vibrant. We either revert back to "I have to pull myself out of this. I have to read my Bible more," or "I am in despair and there is nothing I can do. I will never be who God wants me to be." Christian, do you not understand that Abram's only hope was that God would make him whom God wanted him to be? All Abram does here is get circumcised, and God does everything else. The only thing Abram does accomplishes nothing of earthly value. When you got baptized into the Gospel of Jesus Christ, you were saying, "I cannot climb out of this, but I am also not without hope. Jesus climbed into this for me. Although I cannot be who God wants me to be, he was in my place, and through him, I can be made into that." Abram goes limping out of Genesis 17. We limp, yet what is our hope? Not that we can climb out of it, but that God has climbed down into it for us and is making us new.

The ways in which God makes Jesus real to you, the ways in which he reminds you that he is doing something in you, and the ways in which he reminds you not to go to pride or despair are through the mission and ministry of the local church. Do not forego those means. It is no surprise that so many Christians who are not regularly part of a local church or committed to a local church are in despair. This behavior is like renting a house for your family, never going to the house, and then feeling distant from your family. Abraham lived with a physical reminder that his hope was not in him but in God. You have another physical reminder: the cross of Jesus and the church that brings you to it. Come and see that it is not in us we hope, but rather in the body and blood of Jesus Christ.

Chapter 12

Grace That Finds and Frees Us

Genesis 18:1–15, 21:1–7

The longer that I serve as a pastor, the more I realize that more people identify with Sarah than they do with Abraham. Sarah is someone who is not doing well, not thinking well, and asking questions out of a result of both. It is far easier for most of us to identify with Sarah than with the other so-called heroes of the faith. And if it is easy for us to find ourselves resonating with Sarah, then it should be easy for us to find ourselves resonating with the words God says to Sarah. Let us look at the way God's grace is shown to Sarah, and then ask what are the implications of this grace for our own lives.

How Grace Comes to Us

It is very important that you understand that God is talking to Sarah. There is not a lot going on in this passage, other than Abraham looking off to the distance, seeing three men coming, and going into full cultural hospitality mode. He goes into the tent and tells Sarah to make some cakes and he is going to take care of the meat. Abraham goes and makes sure the provisions are being handled; then he gives the men water and he lets them rest. This is a very cultural thing to do.

Abraham is not the paragon of virtue; he is simply doing what his culture says is required when guests arrive, but we come to find out that these three men are not just any three men, they actually represent God. In a few verses, we are going to see one of them speaking. and Moses writing, "The LORD said ... " (Genesis 18:10a). We also know from the first verse that "the LORD appeared to [Abraham]," so it is clear that God is present. Somehow, and in some way, these three men represent God and speak for God.

Scripture says that God is Spirit (John 4:24a). The Bible also makes it very clear that we should not think of God in terms of any image, so when you think of these three men, you should really think of the burning bush (Exodus 3): Moses sees a bush on fire and sees God speaking from the fire. This burning bush represents the presence of God but is not God. In the same way, these three men represent the presence of God, but they are not God.

Now, you will notice that there is not a lot of direct interaction between God and Sarah in this passage. It would be very easy for us to say, "Well, God is talking to Abraham, not Sarah," but there are a couple of problems with that line of thinking. Number one, God says nothing new here that Abraham doesn't already know. In fact, he says nothing here that he hasn't said to Abraham multiple times and in multiple ways. Number two, we know this because God shows up and asks, "Where is Sarah?" and Abraham replies, "She is in the tent" (Genesis 18:9). After this question, God then says what he is going to do. We know God is speaking to Sarah because the narrator shifts the focus away from the conversation taking place and toward Sarah's inner monologue. Because of this, we are getting a chance to hear what God hears and then see how he responds. Because of these hints, we know that God is coming to talk to Sarah; he's not coming to talk to Abraham.

To understand why this is important, we need to answer the question "Who is Sarah?" First, Sarah is a woman in a culture that devalues women. Why is Sarah in the tent in this passage? Because in this culture, if there were three men who came to visit, the woman did not come out to join them. And not only is she a woman, she is an elderly woman. In fact, we see that she is postmenopausal and in the later stages of life. Not only is Sarah an older woman, she's also a childless woman. Sarah has failed to provide what, in that culture, gives women absolute value: children. Sarah is old, she is a woman, and she is childless. And we see that she has become very cynical, very jaded, and very bitter.

She is, in essence, around the promise of God as Abraham's wife. Abraham received the promise from God, but she has not yet spoken to God. Everything she has is secondhand, and we see here she doesn't believe the promises. When God shows up and says she is going to have a son, she laughs. This is not a comedic laugh; it is not even an external laugh. It is an internal, bitter, and jaded laugh: "Yeah, right. That's going to happen to me." And as if all that is not enough, her relationship with Abraham is not what it used to be. The author writes, "So Sarah laughed to herself saying, 'After I am worn out and my lord is old, shall I have pleasure?" (Genesis 18:12). In the Hebrew, "worn out" literally means "worthless." She is saying, "Not only do I not have children, I can't have children. Abraham is too old and I am too old. How can we have this pleasure?" When you read the word "pleasure," the pleasure you may think of is the pleasure of having a baby and celebrating, but actually, that word, "pleasure," is best translated into sexual pleasure. It is actually a pretty graphic reference in the original language. She's saying, "Oh, sure, God, you are going to do this. I'm a woman, I'm old, I'm childless, and my husband isn't even sleeping with me anymore!"

Why is it so important that we know Sarah's story? Because we need to see that God comes to talk to people just like Sarah. God comes to the old, bitter, jaded, cynical woman whose own husband has forgotten her, and it is so important that we see that because every religion in the world tells us if we do enough good things, we can build a bridge to get to God. Only the God of the Bible, only the God of Christianity, only the God of Genesis 18 says, "A bridge does need to be built, but I'm building it and I'm going to walk across it."

Sarah is in the tent; that's her life. She's not outside, she's not in the promise, and she's not in the story, and if God doesn't show up, she's going to live and die in the tent. She's not coming out on her own to the story. Sarah is not seeking God, and she's definitely not praying. Her day has come and gone, and the promise, up until this point, has passed her by. So many people would identify with Sarah and say, "I'm around God, I'm around the church, and I'm around the Gospel, but I don't feel it. I don't experience it. I'm in the tent, so to speak." And if you come to church enough times, and that is your experience, you will begin to believe that there is a hierarchy to God. You will imagine that God says, "That person in your community group who always hears from God—I love them. I don't love you. That person who is the greater overcomer? I'm teaching them. I won't teach you."

You can begin to believe that, but I want you to see that Sarah is like you! If Sarah were in a community group, she would not be going to community group, spilling her guts. She would not be going to community group and talking about being an overcomer and all that she is learning. She would be going to community group, saying to herself, "I'm bitter and I'm cynical because God said he had a promise for me, and it never came true, and I never got to experience it, and I never got to have it. And everybody tells me I'm worthless, and I feel worthless, and it is like God doesn't even hear me."

And yet, God shows up, and he doesn't show up to talk to Abraham; he shows up to talk to Sarah to get her attention. He doesn't owe that to Sarah. He's God! Sarah could wake up one morning and say, "What's this in my belly? Oh! I'm pregnant!" but God doesn't want the plan to move forward without her; he wants it to move forward with her.

Why is it so important that God won't move forward without Sarah? Because when grace comes, by its very definition, it comes to those who least think they deserve it. It comes to those who are "in the tent"—bitter, cynical, jaded, frustrated—and thinking life has nothing for them. Grace comes to these people. If you are reading this and think, *I'm bitter and frustrated. I'm around the church and I don't get anything. I'm around God and I don't get anything,* please know, it is not because God doesn't care about you, because Sarah is just like you, and yet God shows up.

When he shows up, he sees Sarah not for who she projects herself to be but for exactly who she is! On the outside, Sarah is doing everything that a woman in this culture is supposed to do: She makes the cakes, and then she makes herself scarce. Sarah is doing everything right! If you were to show up and see this, you might think, "Man, this is a great woman. She's supportive and she believes all this." She could fool everybody, but she couldn't fool God.

God sees her laughing inside the tent. This isn't Sarah laughing out loud at the punch line of a good joke. She's laughing on the inside. And God sees right through her! He sees into her bitterness, cynicism, doubt, and insecurity, and yet he still comes for her! Grace, by its very definition, is God coming to us, not us going to God. Grace is also God coming to the real us. We can never experience grace until we say to God, "This is who I really am. This is where I'm really at." Many of us are like Sarah and only speak to God in inner monologue. We have all these conversations with ourselves, but we don't bring God into any of them. We are so afraid that if we are really honest, he is going to destroy us.

But after Sarah's laughter, we come to one of the most beautiful parts of Genesis 18:1–15. God asks why she laughs, and she replies, "I didn't laugh," to which he replies, "Oh, but you did laugh" (Genesis 18:14–15). God knows exactly who she is, but he says, "I know exactly who you are, Sarah, and yet I'm telling you, I'm going to do something." After Sarah laughs, God asks her, "Is anything too hard for the Lord?" Many of our Bibles will footnote the word "hard" and down at the bottom will give an alternate translation as "wonderful."

Sarah's problem is more than biological. Sarah is saying, "If things like this happen, they don't happen to people like me. Nothing wonderful happens to me!" And God is responding by saying, "Is anything too wonderful for me? Sarah, do you not see? Can you ponder? Can you open yourself up to the possibility that there really is nothing too wonderful for me?"

So many of us are like Sarah. We go to community group and we say, "Pray for me; I'm so busy." Underneath the busyness, layers lower, is the unspoken prayer request "I'm also frustrated. I'm so angry! And I don't understand what God's doing!" We're afraid to get to that level, yet here's the truth: If God is God, he already hears all that, so for me to go to community group and say, "I'm busy, pray for me," is not wonderful, but for me to show up and say, "This is where I'm really at" and for people to love me and pray for me on that level is wonderful. God is saying to Sarah, "My grace means I know who you are and yet I'm still going to do something wonderful."

If you are not a Christian, God's not asking you to pretend to be anything that you are not. Rather, honestly consider what the Gospel is saying. Be yourself and show up to community group and say, "I don't believe any of this. Here's my problem. My objection is this ... !" Sarah had questions, and God cared about them. We are seeking to give you a place where you can see God for who he really is while being who you really are.

If you are a Christian, don't push the questioning types away. Being a Sarah is a seasonal thing. You go through times when you are bitter, cynical, and frustrated. Nobody wants to be around those people, but they are the exact people God cares about. These are the people with whom God shows up to talk. We can't be a church that pushes people away and says, "You ask too many questions." Sarah was our model doubter, and yet God showed up to her.

What Happens When Grace Comes to Us

God is saying to Sarah, "Listen, if you will just take a small step, I'll show you I'm wonderful." In other words, grace comes to her first, and then God asks her for a small step of faith. Sarah exclaims, "We're not even sleeping together anymore!" and God says, "Listen, I'm going to do this." A good translation is "Start sleeping together! Take a step of faith." When God comes to us in grace, he asks us to take a small step, to open up to him and say, "Okay, I'm willing to consider that you can do anything. There is nothing too wonderful for you." God says to Sarah, "Start living as though you are going to have a child. Start doing those things, and you'll see!"

What would he say to you today? For some of you it is "Go to a community group! You are never are going to know that I love you and care about you until you can sit in a room full of people and be who you exactly are and have them love and care about you—not because they're good people, but because they know my love and my care. And as they show it to you, you'll know it is real."

Some of you come to Q&A time following the service and God says, "You've got a question. Just take a step and believe that maybe I've got an answer to that question." For some of you, God says to meet with a pastor and say, "Hey, this is who I am and what I'm going through. How does God speak into this?" When grace comes to us, it says to us, "Take a small step." What is that small step? It is simply opening up to the idea that there really is nothing too wonderful for God. Sarah does it. She begins to sleep with her husband again. She gets pregnant and she has a child. And then look at what Genesis 21:1 says: "The Lord visited Sarah as he had said, and the Lord did to Sarah as he had promised."

All of this is God-initiated. If God had never come to Sarah, she never would have even considered having a child. If God hadn't heard her inner monologue and spoken into it, she would never have tried to conceive. If God hadn't asked, "Is anything too wonderful?" she never would have stepped out in faith. If you think, *Well then, I have to be like Sarah. I have to dig down to a dark place and release all my bitterness, all my frustration, all my cynicism, all my doubt, and just believe!* you're wrong. The emphasis is not on the grace receiver; it is on the grace giver! It's not on Sarah; it's on the God who said, "I'm gonna do this, even if you don't believe me; even if you are laughing. I'm gonna do this." The emphasis is on God. This first step you take is to say, "I'm like Sarah. I'm never going to get out of this unless you show up, so I'll pray that you'll show up."

Genesis 21:2–6 says, "And Sarah conceived and bore Abraham a son in his old age at the time which God had spoken to him. Abraham called the name of his son who was born to him, whom Sarah bore him, Isaac. And Abraham circumcised his son Isaac when he was eight days old, as God had commanded him. Abraham was a hundred years old when his son Isaac was born to him. And Sarah said, 'God has made laughter for me; everyone who hears will laugh over me.'" The name Isaac literally means "He laughs." Why did they name him Isaac? Because when God told Abraham he would have a son, he laughed. When God told Sarah she would have a son, she laughed. God's saying, "This is the child of laughter, the one you both didn't think could happen. The answer to the question 'Is anything too wonderful for me?' is no! He's called Isaac; you can laugh about this." Sarah says, "God has me laugh! He's given me a reason to be joyful!" Sarah is still a laugher, but what has changed is the drive behind the laughter. It is no longer a bitter, cynical laugh—it's a joyful laugh. Why? Because God has taken her from worthless to having worth. God has taken her from the tent and into the story.

Grace has transformed the bitter and cynical kind of laugh to laughter for all the right reasons. Sarah lived her whole life under the shame of her culture. She had no value because she was a woman without children. She was old, and the time to have children had passed. She was completely and utterly worthless, and look what she says: "God has made laughter for me; everyone who hears will laugh over me." This can be translated as "Everyone will mock me and everyone will scorn me." She knows this, but she doesn't care. Her whole life, she's been subject to what the culture has said. Her desire to have worth even drove her to take another woman and give that woman to her husband and say, "Sleep with her! Just end this! Put me out of my misery! Give me a son," and even that didn't work. Here, she's saying,

"Now the same people who laughed at me before are going to laugh at me again. The only difference is I don't care. Grace has freed me. I know I'm somebody because I'm not in the tent. I'm in the story, so who cares who laughs? They only laugh because they don't know the story."

The difference here is not entirely circumstantial. People are still going to mock her, scorn her, and laugh at her. They're not going to believe Sarah had a child of her own. But she says it doesn't matter. "I'm going to laugh out of joy because of what God has done, because I know that I was real with God, I was honest with God. He saw me anyway. He loved me anyway. And I know nothing is too wonderful for God, because I'm holding a son. Nobody else knew this was going to happen. Everybody thought, *This is too wonderful to happen!*"

Sarah remembers what it was like a year ago in the tent. She knows God heard her. She knows she did more than laugh. She knows she lied to God by saying, "I didn't laugh." The very last thing she said to God before Isaac was a lie. Sarah was really seen and really heard and yet truly loved. That's grace. Grace comes to us and says, "You can be who you really are. It doesn't mean I'm going to leave you there. I hear you, see you, and love you—and I'm going to change you." She's experienced grace, and it has changed her. She doesn't care what people say. She doesn't see her insecurities and her weaknesses as impediments to God. Nothing's too wonderful for God. If we can believe that God can really see us and really hear us and yet really love us, grace will change us.

The One through Whom Grace Comes

All this is a great story and it's a great passage, but it doesn't mean anything until Sarah's holding Isaac. Until she's holding Isaac, she thinks, *God hears me; he sees me, but he doesn't keep his promises. He doesn't love me.* It is not until she holds Isaac that she realizes, "This whole time, God saw me. This whole time, God heard me. This whole time, God loved me." It is the presence of her son that tells her these things are true. A woman who should not be having children and gives birth to a child promised by God obviously points us forward to the Gospels, where another woman who should not be having children has a child. Mary is not too old; she is a virgin when she conceives Jesus. And that child is the son of God, and is God with us. Do you see how God showing up at Sarah's tent, saying, "Sarah, you're never gonna get to me, but I've come to you," is the exact same as God in the person of Jesus saying to all of us through his birth, "You're never gonna get to me, but I've come to you"?

Every other religion says, "Be good enough, and maybe you'll get to God." Only Christianity says, "God looked down and came to us." God comes to us in the person of Jesus. And to whom does Jesus come when he begins his ministry? He goes around preaching and looking for the Sarahs. Everywhere he goes, he's looking for the weak and broken. He says things like "It's not the healthy who need a doctor, but the sick" (Mark 2:17) and that his purpose is to "seek and save the lost" (Luke 19:10). He's saying, "I hear their inner monologue and I know their insecurity and doubt." He knows when he talks with these people that their only hope is that nothing is too wonderful for God. When he goes to the wealthy religious crowd and asks, "What if nothing is too wonderful for God?" they all respond, "I don't know, Jesus, it's pretty wonderful here. What if God just left us alone?" Jesus resonates with the Sarahs of the world who are in the tents of their lives and saying, "I don't believe any of this. I'm around it, but I never get it. Nothing wonderful ever happens for me. This is never going to make sense for me. This is never going to happen to me." And here comes Jesus. He's showing up. He's showing people grace, and he's changing them. Remember the story of woman at the well? She runs back to her town after meeting Jesus, and she says, "Come see a man who told me all that I ever did" (John 4:29a). The implication is simple. She is saying, "Come see the man who knows everything about me that you know about me and yet loves me. He hears me and he sees me, and he loves me." That's what Jesus does. He spends his whole life hearing people, seeing people, and loving people.

We tend to push difficult people away. We don't like messy, and we don't like people who bring too many questions. Yet Jesus never pushes those people way. He shows up to a whole town and heals hundreds of people. He's everything you and I are not. He's never in the tent. He's always in the story. He's never bitter, although he has every right to be. He's never cynical, although he has every right to be. He loves all the Sarahs. He never pushes them away. When Sarah looks at Isaac, she knows God loves her, and all she has is a little piece of a promise: a baby. But God's promise to Abraham is not "You shall have a baby."

They have to still look forward, to when Jesus comes and goes to the cross. On the cross, he's paying for all the frustration and all the bitterness and all the cynicism of the church—all those who would turn to him. Sarah hears God's promise in Isaac: "You've got the down payment; you have to wait for the rest." On the cross, Jesus says, "It is finished" (John 19:30). We look at Sarah and think, *If God would just show up to me and give me a sign like that, I would believe,* but we have something far better than one baby, who really only points to many babies to come. We have God in the flesh, nailed to the cross, saying, "It is finished."

"Is anything too wonderful for God?" Our only hope is that God answered that question finally and ultimately on the cross. Our only hope is that we come to the cross exactly as we are, just as God came to Sarah. Our hope is that God sees us exactly who we are and that all the sinfulness, the wickedness, and the insecurity residing in our hearts is put on Jesus on the cross and when Jesus says, "It is finished," he means God has wiped it away so that when we come to God, God can build us up and make us new just like Sarah is made new. That's the Gospel. The Gospel is believing that God became a man and walked among us and saw us for who we really are and went to the cross to pay for who we really are.

The cross is saying that the answer to the question "Is anything too wonderful for me?" is no. The work is finished, and Jesus rises from the dead and says to us, "If you'll trust in me, then all of your inner monologue can be put on me and you can get a new inner monologue—one that leads to laughter not from bitterness but from joy."

If you classify yourself as something other than a Christian, this is the Gospel message for you: Like Sarah, believe that God can hear exactly what's going on in your heart and yet he still loves you and he's still willing to show you that nothing is too wonderful for him. The only reason Christians are laughing for joy is not because we read the right book or pulled ourselves up by our bootstraps but rather because God showed up and said, "Watch and see how wonderful I really am." That's our hope. You can say to God, "God, if you can show up and show me you're wonderful in the person of Jesus, I'll take it." Sarah did that. She wasn't disappointed.

If you're a Christian, you have to fight against resisting the Sarahs. In our own ranks, it is the believer who shows up to community group and doesn't have the right answers—the one who hasn't had a great week, the one struggling with doubt or insecurity. Don't you see we have to love them? Don't you see we have to show them that God builds a bridge and comes to them? Don't you see that we have to remind them that Jesus dealt with the insecurity they're dealing with toward the past, the insecurity they're dealing with in the moment, and the insecurity they're going to deal with in the future? Don't you see that when you recoil and you say, "Why can't I go to the community group where everybody's healthy and everybody's good?" you wouldn't belong there and that's the exact opposite of our mission? We serve the God who said, "It's not the healthy who need a doctor, but the sick," the one who comes to seek and save that which was lost.

Until you and I come to see that we really are just like Sarah and that God's grace is our only hope, we'll never really be able to extend that hope to other people. We can talk all we want about making Jesus famous, but Jesus is made famous when he changes the inner monologue of those in the tent and brings them into the story. We are those people in the tent, and we can be brought into the story not by our own strength, but rather by what God has done for us.

Chapter 13

The One Who Removes Absurdity from Faith

Genesis 22:1–19

Abraham was one of the most important men to ever live. He is universally recognized as a man of great faith and a man to whom all people of faith might look—and here we come to probably the most significant moment in his life. Most people when they think of Abraham will think of the story of Abraham and Isaac, a story that is in both the Bible and the Qur'an. It is the crowning moment of an incredible life.

On face value, this is a story full of many absurdities. The first absurdity is the idea that God would say to a man, "Sacrifice your son." The second absurdity is the man listening. If you don't know what is coming, when you read the story, you would be incredulous at both God and Abraham, yet there is a third absurdity; when we hear this story, we may come away thinking we need to be like Abraham. It is absurd that anyone would think they should emulate Abraham's actions.

Many of us view faith as absurd. The idea that a God asks things like this is absurd. The notion that we are supposed to go along with it and abandon everything in pursuit of this God is incredibly absurd. But if we look at this story carefully, we can see that God uses Abraham to teach us something incredible about the nature of faith and how we reconcile that faith with the absurdity of this story. This story has something incredible to teach us about the nature of faith, whether you are something other than a Christian and say this story is the exact reason you are not interested in the Bible or you are a Christian struggling with the idea of faith. It will teach us something challenging, sobering, and inspiring. It teaches us about who God is, who we are, and how those two things can be reconciled.

The Call of Faith

"After these things, God tested Abraham" (Genesis 22:1a). It is important to see the word test in the first verse. This is a test. When you read this passage, the first reaction is, "What kind of a God asks a man to give his own son?" The reality is, in this passage, the writer shows us the story in two dimensions. We see the story through the lens of Abraham, with his limited knowledge and understanding, but we also have the second dimension of understanding why God is doing what he is doing. This is a test, a challenge. We know that because God ultimately steps in and stops Abraham from carrying through with the sacrifice. This fact does not mitigate our visceral reaction to it, nor should it. Abraham does not know it is a test; he really thinks this is happening. We should read it that way and feel what Abraham feels. We should not stop asking the question "What kind of a God does this?" but we should change the question into a more specific one: "What kind of a God gives this kind of a test?"

The Bible is abundantly clear that God is against child sacrifice. It is a part of the Old Testament law that this is a capital offense (Deuteronomy 12:31). Israel lived among many groups who would sacrifice children and bury them under the cornerstones of their houses to get their god Moloch to bless them. The Bible makes it clear in the law given by Moses that God detests this. Abraham does not know any of that yet. He does not know about the nation of Israel, or what the law is going to be. He does not know God is going to make child sacrifice a capital offense. God is not in favor of child sacrifice, but he gives the test nonetheless. This leads to the question "If God is not seeking child sacrifice, then why give this test?" But a better question would be "What is this test designed to illustrate?"

To answer that question, we look at another test from an even older book of the Bible, Job. Satan argues with God that Job's faith is an accessory to his life because Job has everything he could want from God. God offers Satan to take anything he can away from Job to show that Job's faith is built on his affection for God, not for the things God has given him (Job 1). Job loses everything, but at the end of the book, he says it is enough to simply know God, and Satan is proven wrong (Job 42).

Abraham understands faith in the same way as Job. One theologian has described faith as putting down one thing and picking up another, namely God. When God first came to Abraham, God told Abraham to leave his family, his homeland, his security, and his culture to go to a place God is going to show him. He was telling Abraham that the call of faith is to put down everything and follow God. He was telling Abraham to believe that God is better and more essential than anything else Abraham has. Abraham heard, and he went. (Genesis 12)

God showed up the first time and said, "Give up everything you have for the hope of something I am promising you." This time, when God comes to Abraham, he issues the same call: "Take all that you possess and believe that I am better than that." The first time, Abraham did not have much to leave behind, but this time, Abraham has a son; he has seen God deliver on his promise with this son. The Bible makes abundantly clear that the call of faith is to put everything down and to pick God up. You hear this when Jesus says the whole law of God can be summed up in one verse: "Love the LORD your God with all your heart and with all your soul and with all your mind" (Matthew 22:37). You see this fleshed out in the story of Jesus and the rich young ruler. Jesus tells the man he has to put down his identity as the rich young ruler and pick up the poor follower of Jesus. The ruler wants to accessorize Jesus and faith. He wants to be the rich young faithful ruler. Jesus says the other adjectives are to be dropped and the man is to be just the young faithful guy. (Mark 10:17–27).

We see in Abraham's story that God requires absolute devotion in faith. We can treat faith like it is an addition to our homes. God is saying to Abraham once again, "Leave everything and follow me." We wonder how Abraham could do it, but this is how he met God in the first place. For Abraham, faith meant giving up everything to follow God; for us, it means giving up an hour on Sunday mornings. You cannot understand the story or the Bible unless you understand that God requires absolute devotion.

According to the Bible, you certainly can grow in faith, but you cannot say, "Part of me is dedicated to my faith." The call on Abraham is "Give up everything. Follow me." We do not recoil at this story only because the idea of sacrificing a child nauseates us. That is part of it, but we also recoil from a God who would dare to ask for something so precious. In our lives, we have a portion of things God takes—ten percent of our money, a portion of our weeks, or some volunteer hours—but he cannot ask for something like this. When we recoil, we oftentimes are recoiling at the idea of a God who wants us to put things down to pick him up, but that is the call of faith.

What does the call of faith cost Abraham? It costs his son. There is surprisingly little emotion in the story of Abraham and Isaac, leading us to ask, "Does not Abraham care about his son?" He does. Look at what God says to Abraham when he talks to him first in verse 2. God repeats himself four different ways when he speaks:

1. Take your son

2. Your only son

3. Isaac

4. Whom you love

Most scholars acknowledge that when God says, "Take your son," he is saying, "Please, take your son." The presence of the implied "please" indicates that God knows the scope of what he is asking. Most scholars also believe the reason the writer does not tell us of Abraham's emotion is because the best way for us to feel the weight of the emotion is to leave it absent so we can substitute our own emotion. In verse 6, when they are climbing up the mountain and they have said good-bye to the servants, Abraham puts the wood on Isaac to carry, and Abraham carries in his hand the fire and the knife. Even as they are walking up the mountain, where he is going to kill his own son, Abraham says to Isaac, "You take the wood; I will carry the dangerous things." Even on the way up the mountain, Abraham is looking out for Isaac. He loves Isaac. He has a son, he has his wife back, he has joy, and he has an identity.

Isaac represents more than just a boy for Abraham. If Abraham does not have Isaac, then what was the point of the last twenty-five years of his life? All the travels, all the struggles, and all the dangers he has been through do not make sense without Isaac. Not only does the past not make sense if Isaac dies, but his present does not make sense. Killing Isaac kills Abraham's religion. He does not have any promise from God at this point. If he kills Isaac, how will Isaac become a nation? If Isaac does not become a nation, how will Abraham's descendants increase? If his descendants do not increase, how do they bless the nations? God is asking for more than a son, he is asking for Abraham's whole identity.

The Crisis of Faith

If all this is true, why would Abraham do it? This is the crisis of faith: God asks for everything; we do not want to give everything. For Abraham, everything is represented in Isaac. Everything he has is bound up in Isaac. Why would Abraham give up everything? The answer is in verse 2, where God says, "Take your son, your only son Isaac, whom you love, and go to the land of Moriah, and offer him there as a burnt offering." We know from Scripture that a burnt offering is the offering for sin (Leviticus 1:3–9).

The story of Abraham is not the story of us finding a good example. He is not an example of moral virtue. God shows up and says, "Oh, one last thing before moving forward. ... Do you know you have sin?" Abraham says, "Yes, God, I do." And the payment for his sin is Isaac. He goes up the mountain because he knows he is a sinner; he has a deep and abiding sense of God's justice. Throughout the Bible, the firstborn of the family represents the family's hope in future promises. In pagan religions, the firstborn would be sacrificed, but in the Bible, God would develop a process for redeeming the firstborn (Exodus 13:2). Again, Abraham does not know any of this, as none of God's law has been developed yet, but we are beginning to see the theme developed as God is saying, "Your sin is so great, I require of you the best you have as payment—your son, Isaac."

Just a few chapters earlier, Abraham was arguing with God, negotiating with God on behalf of Sodom and Gomorrah, a city of serial rapists, where the rich ignored and trampled over the poor. It was a very evil city (Genesis 18:16–33). Abraham was so bold with God there, but here, he does not do any arguing with God. It was easy for Abraham to assume that maybe there are ten righteous people in Sodom and Gomorrah, but when he looked in his own heart, he knew there was no one righteous within. Abraham has a deep, abiding sense of God's justice and a deep, abiding sense of his own sinfulness. He knows his whole story has been God giving him things he does not deserve. Every time he looks at Isaac, he knows about Hagar and Ishmael. Why does God call Isaac his only son? Because he threw his last son out. He knows who he is, and he knows who God is. Abraham has been bracing for this collision. When God shows up and says it is time to make payment, Abraham cannot ignore his sin anymore. God requires his son. And when we read this story and ask how God could require anything like this, we do not understand something that

Abraham did. He understands God has a deep and abiding sense of justice.

The crisis of faith happens when God shows up and says, "Give me everything." We inevitably worry about what happens if we do give God everything. Abraham believes something different. He sees God saying, "Give up everything, but if you give up Isaac especially, you will have no sin. I will make you right and I will be reconciled to you. I will be in relationship with you." The crisis of faith is God saying to Abraham, "Give everything up, but if you do, we will be right." The problem is that we hear about the call of faith to give up everything and trust in God, and we say it is too much to give up, which brings us to an existential crisis. We say, "I do not want to give everything up; that sounds crazy to me," yet the more I understand who God is and the more I understand who I am, I see I have a tremendous debt I owe to God. I have spent my whole life in rebellion to God, hurting God and hurting people, living in sin and saying I am God. When God asks Abraham, "Are you a sinner?" by demanding a sacrifice, Abraham does not argue like he argued over Sodom and Gomorrah. He knows the answer. God says, "Offer your son as a burnt offering." In a burnt offering, you would take an animal, put the animal on the altar, kill it, and burn it up completely. That animal would represent your sin. God says to Abraham that his son is going to be the animal. In obeying, Abraham says he believes that his sin is enough to deserve this punishment.

If you would ask Abraham, "How could you believe in a God who asks for that?" Abraham would say that is the wrong question. He would ask, "How could you look at my life and not believe that I deserve that?"

This crisis of sin and sacrifice is the beginning of understanding faith. When you first understand that God wants everything—career, money, time, and affection—your first thought is *no*, but when you look closely at your life and think, *The only thing I do not have in moderation is my rebellion against God. What if giving up everything could make that right?* That is the existential crisis to which we must come. If you find religious people doing religious things and you ask, "Why are you doing this?" they will probably reply, "I have a huge debt to pay, and my only hope is that the more I give up, the more that debt goes away."

If you have not struggled your way to faith, you do not have faith. If you hear the call to give up everything and immediately say, "Okay, I give it up," then you did not really give it up. If you say, "I will not give up anything. That is not what faith requires," then you do not understand the call or the debt you owe. Abraham fought for Sodom and Gomorrah, but he does not fight for himself; he knows who he is. Do you know who you are? Do you honestly think that when the real you and the real God collide, it is going to be a pleasant experience? Fortunately for us, this story is not only about the call of faith or the crisis of faith but is also about the courage of faith.

The Courage of Faith

Abraham shows tremendous courage moving forward here. Where does that courage come from? Most people who preach this passage will say you should be like Abraham: If you climb the proverbial mountain of faith, the debt will be paid. But that is not what is happening here. Abraham's courage is not an internal reality. Abraham does not summon up any inner reservoir of courage. Instead, the beginning of verse 7 tells us, "Isaac said to his father to Abraham, 'My Father!' And he said, 'Here I am, my son.'" Isaac is beginning to put two and two together, but he doesn't know all the implications. Abraham knows fully what they are going up the mountain to do. Then Isaac continues to speak: "Behold, the fire and the wood, but where is the lamb for the burnt offering?" He is really asking, "Daddy, who is going to pay for your sin? You have to bring an animal, don't you? Somebody has to pay for this."

Remember that at this point, Abraham doesn't know this is a test. Who does he think is going to pay for his sin? Look at what he says:

"God will provide for himself the lamb for a burnt offering, my son,"
(Genesis 22:8a). The word "provide" here literally means "God will see
to it." Abraham is saying, "God will see to there being a lamb for the
burnt offering, my son." Despite the crisis of this situation, Abraham is
going up the mountain with courage, but his courage is not in himself; his courage is in the hope that God will provide. How do we
know this? Look at what Abraham says to his servants in verse 5: "Stay
here with the donkey; I and the boy will go over there and worship
and come again to you." He tells the servants that both he and his son
will come back. How can he say that? He does not know how yet, but
he believes.

The writer of the book of Hebrews will tell us that Abraham believes
that even if he goes to the mountain and kills Isaac, God will raise
Isaac from the dead (Hebrews 11:17). Abraham believes that his only
hope is in God both making and keeping his promises. Why does
Abraham believe in such a God?

Do you remember when God tells Abraham to get some animals, cut
them in half, and spread them out? When Abraham cuts the animals
and spreads them out, he falls asleep and God passes through instead
of Abraham. God was saying to Abraham at that moment, "Abraham,
here is your hope—not that if you do not keep the deal, you will be
ripped apart, but rather if I do not keep the deal, I will be ripped
apart." (See Genesis 15 or Chapter 10 of this book for more details.)

Abraham goes up the mountain saying, "I have no idea what God is
doing or how he is doing it. I have no idea what will happen next, but
I do know God keeps his promises. God will raise Isaac from the dead
if he must. Isaac is not going to stay dead." He goes up the mountain
to give Isaac to God, fully expecting to get Isaac back, because God
has proven to him that he is good.

Abraham is teaching us that the only way we can hear the call of faith
and push through the crisis of faith into actually knowing God and
believing God is if God has in the past done something so great that

we are utterly convinced of God's goodness, even if we don't know what is coming next. God knows what he is doing, and he has proven he is for us, not against us.

Abraham was not trusting himself; he was trusting God. He had courage because in his past, God, not Abraham, passed through the animals. Abraham's courage is not internal. I cannot tell you to have the courage of Abraham, because unless God has done something in the past to show you he is for you, you can never have this kind of courage.

Thankfully, you don't have to climb mountains with your children. You have something so much better than that. This story points forward to another father and another son: God the Father and God the Son. When Isaac asks Abraham, "Daddy, where is the lamb?" it sounds like another son in a garden, praying, "If there is any other way, let us do it that way" (Luke 22:42). Today, many of us say, "God should not have asked for Isaac," but Abraham does not say that, and it is his very own son. It is not our Isaac; it is Abraham's Isaac. Abraham does not say that, because he knows his sin is great. Abraham has no choice; it is what his sin requires, until God steps in and says, "Do not do it."

Another son cried out to his father, but for him, nobody stopped the knife. God does not require Abraham to kill Isaac because the death of Isaac accomplishes nothing. He took on this task himself in Jesus. God says to us, "Do you see your sin is great? It is. But to show you that I am worth giving up everything, I am going to do away with your debt not by requiring something of you. I will require it of myself." Abraham goes up the mountain, thinking he is going to have to pay everything, but in the end, he actually pays nothing. On the cross, when Jesus died for our sin, we also gave up nothing. How can we have the courage to step forward and give God everything? How do we trust that he loves us and will not hurt us? God says the only way we can trust like Abraham is if we know he has done something in the past to prove it. And he has proven it on the cross.

The Gospel says you do not come to God and say, "I will give you everything. Please show me you are there." Rather, you look at what God has already done. Abraham was not driven by what he thought God might be doing or by goose bumps or spiritual highs. He was driven by what God had already done. So are we. God says to Abraham, "Now I know you love me because you would not withhold your only son" (Genesis 22:12). Today, we look to the cross and say to God, "Now we know you love us, because you would not withhold your only son."

Do not go to church and say, "If I do not get goose bumps, God does not love me." We have a past-tense, foundational relationship with God. We look to what God has done. Do not worry about goose bumps or a lack of goose bumps. Look at what God has done. Paul will say ask if God did not spare his own son, why would we not assume that he is out for our good (Romans 8:32)? Whatever God is calling you to do, if you are worried that you do not have the courage, rest assured, you are not meant to have enough courage. You are meant to say, "I have no idea what is going on, but here is my only hope: God went to the cross for me and gave up his own son and raised him from the dead. If he did that for me, I know he is not calling me to move forward just so he can crush me. Rather, I know he loves me; I know he is for me. Even though I do not have the answer, I am moving forward."

Jesus Christ removes the absurdity from faith. We can go back over 2,000 years ago to a cross, and we see the Son crying out, and we see the Father swinging the knife, but the knife does not stop. The Son is killed for our sin and for our judgment. Now, when God raises him from the dead, he can say to us, "I love you. Believe me. Follow me. Give up everything for me." The whole way up the mountain, Abraham had no idea about his future. He was giving up everything to God, but he got it all back. When you give up everything to God, you are not disappointed.

As Christians, we are not called to look to Abraham as a model for our faith. Rather, we are to look to the same one to whom Abraham looked: Jesus, the son who was killed for us in order that we might be reconciled to God. It is only through Jesus that we can know God is for us.

Chapter 14

A Stairway to Heaven:
Our Need for a Personal Experience
of God's Grace

Genesis 28:10–22

The Bible can be understood as the unfolding of God's sovereign grace in human history. It can be compared to a missile. In Genesis 3, God launches the missile by promising to send someone to make the world right. He promises to make the world right through his sovereign grace. The promise is neither conditional nor based on anything anyone else is going to do. All the Scriptures are the unfolding of that promise to bring about cosmic renewal.

But that is not all the Bible is. Genesis 28 is in the Bible so we can know that while God is interested in cosmic renewal, he is also interested in personal renewal. Jacob is not a pawn in God's overall plan of sovereign grace; he is a person. God does not see Jacob as an instrument or a tool but as a person. God desires to know Jacob as a person, and he desires to show sovereign grace, renewal, and restoration both in the world and in Jacob's personal life.

There are two reasons we need to hear that. First, it is much safer to talk about cosmic renewal than it is to talk about personal renewal; therefore, we have a bias toward cosmic renewal. Everybody gets excited about cosmic renewal, even people who do not trust Jesus. As a society, we talk constantly about justice, taking care of the marginalized, and crossing ethnic lines or national lines. These are easy to talk about, but the Bible is concerned with more than that. We cannot look at the Bible only from 30,000 feet. We cannot see God's sovereign grace as only a universal thing; we have to see it as personal. The temptation is to keep God's sovereign grace at a safe distance, but that is not where the Bible is calling us, specifically in Genesis 28. Jacob's dream only matters if God cares about not only cosmic renewal but also personal renewal. We cannot simply view God as an entity who is doing things out there, but also as a God who is standing at the door of our hearts, saying, "I desire to renew and restore you." That is what Jacob experiences, and that is what we have to experience.

In any relationship, we do not get to define the other person. So it is with God. If we want to know him, we cannot reduce him down to the one dimension that we like; we have to deal with him in a three-dimensional, holistic way. If God desires both cosmic renewal and personal renewal, we have to deal with him on that level. We have to accept or reject God on that level. We cannot say we only like the cosmic, global God but do not want to talk about what that means for our own lives. It is not enough to know God has a plan based on his sovereign grace; we also need to know it is a personal plan. We need a personal experience of God's sovereign grace.

Jacob and his dream help us understand what it means to personally experience this grace. The Bible includes this story so we know that Jacob not just is part of God's sovereign plan but also experiences God's sovereign grace. To unpack the story, we will approach the narrative in four ways:

1. the setting of Jacob's dream

2. the subject of Jacob's dream

3. the effect of Jacob's dream

4. the source of Jacob's dream

By way of background, we need to understand Jacob is not a great guy. First, he cheats his older brother, Esau, out of Esau's inheritance with some stew. Then, he manipulates and lies to his blind, dying father by pretending to be that very same older brother. Esau then wants to kill Jacob, so his mother and father send Jacob to find a wife to save him from his brother. Jacob is on a journey to his mother's family. He comes to a place of rest when the sun goes down, and he is about to fall asleep.

Do we see where Jacob is relationally? He has only one brother, that wants to kill him. By the way, that brother is a hunter. He has a father who, after begrudgingly blessing him, is sending him away. Isaac still prefers Esau. Jacob has a mother who loves him, but even she knows she has to send him away. The only person on the whole planet who loves him is his mother, and he will never see her again.

Where is Jacob physically? He is wandering in the wilderness and has come to a place without a name, sign, or significant landmark. There is nothing here. The only reason he stays here is because the sun is going down. He realizes he has to sleep, so he sleeps on a rock. You only sleep with your head on a rock when you do not have anything, and Jacob has nothing. This is a beautiful way the author is saying Jacob is nowhere, has nothing, and has no one. That is the context of his dream.

Jacob's dream is an interruption to his life. Jacob would have nothing if not for a plan. He is traveling over to his mother's family, where he is going to find a wife. Jacob does not pray; he does not seek God's will. He just does. If he wants something, he cheats, lies, and steals to get it. He is an ends-justify-the-means kind of guy. But here, he has nothing and he goes to sleep. The author is telling us that everything about to happen has nothing to do with Jacob's efforts. God is going to intrude, interrupt, and say, "Jacob! I know you think you have something going on, but we are working on a new plan now. I have something I want you to do."

You could call this intrusion wonderfully hostile. It is hostile because when God shows up, he does not give Jacob options. It is wonderfully hostile because it is good news. Every time we see God show up in Genesis, the person in whose life God intrudes is going nowhere spiritually. Every time God shows up, he interrupts, he intrudes, and he is hostile. He says, "Here is my plan. Here is what we are going to do." He is wonderful, but every time he reveals himself, it is not the result of people seeking him but instead the result of him seeking those people. As we read on and Jacob becomes a great figure, Genesis 28 wants to show that Jacob's transformation was really God interrupting with sovereign grace.

We are just like Jacob. We cannot understand experiencing grace until we understand we are all like Jacob: we are nowhere, we have nothing, and we have no one. We think we are not like Jacob, but metaphorically and spiritually, we are.

Every great person that you find in the Bible is only that way because God interrupted, God intruded, and God interceded. They had plans, and God showed up and said, "No, we are not going to do that; we are going to do this."

Not only is Jacob not seeking God, but God knows this and in a really beautiful way drives this point home. The author writes in verse 12: "And he dreamed and behold there was a ladder." "Ladder" is not the best translation. The original word is only used one other time in the Old Testament, but it really conveys more the idea of a stairway. One of the ways you see that is because multiple angels are going up and down it. That is difficult to do with a ladder. Most commentators agree there is a stairway and the top of it reaches to heaven. The other time we see this word is in Genesis 11, when the people of the earth get together and are going to build the tower of Babel all the way up to heaven. They are saying, "If we build this tower, we are going to be able to climb up to heaven and we will be like God."

In Genesis 28, God shows up with the same exact structure from Genesis 11. He is saying, not to Jacob, but to us, "If you think you will seek and find me, if you think you will build a tower and get to me, you are wrong. The only way we can communicate is if I build the tower. The tower does not go bottom-up, but top-down. It goes from me to you, not from you to me. Do not think I do not desire to be known personally. Just know I have to build the tower; you cannot build it. I have to come down; you cannot come up." So God shows up and says, "Jacob, you are not seeking me. You are never going to seek me, but I am seeking you. Even though you are a nobody in nowhere with no one, I am showing up and am interrupting and giving you a new plan to follow."

When we personally experience the sovereign grace of God, we experience it as an interruption, as an intrusion. It disrupts our plans. It disrupts who we are. If it has not, we have not experienced the grace of God. Every time God's sovereign grace interrupts or intrudes into a person's life, it completely and utterly changes that person. It devastates them in an incredibly wonderful way. It devastates who they thought they were and what they thought they were doing, but it builds something greater in return. It may be true that one of the things Genesis 28 is teaching us is that we are never in line more to experience the grace of God than when we come to grips with the fact that we are nowhere, with nothing and no one. The secret to finding the tower that connects man with God is not by trying to build your way up to God but rather by sleeping on a rock in the middle of nowhere. The mechanism for experiencing the grace of God is to say, "I do not know what I am doing spiritually. I do not know how I could ever get to God," and to beg for God to reach out to you, interrupt, and be wonderfully hostile in your life. Jacob does not become part of what

God is doing until God interrupts, intrudes, and intercedes. He is around what God is doing, but he is not a part of the story until God shows up. The first step for us to discover God is to say to God, "Intrude. Interrupt. Intercede. Be wonderfully hostile. Show up. Devastate what I have going on. Build something new."

God shows up in the dream in verse 13: "And behold, the LORD stood above it and said, 'I am the LORD, the God of Abraham your father and the God of Isaac.'" God shows up because Jacob does not know what is going on. God is giving Jacob context. The last time Jacob saw Isaac, he cheated him and lied to him. God shows up and says, "I am the God of the guy you cheated." Jacob would have heard that and been nervous. When God shows up and says, "I am the God of Isaac," we expect him to also say, "I am going to destroy you." God is giving Jacob context and saying, "Jacob, what you deserve from me is judgment." When God intrudes and intercedes in people's lives, the first step is to give them context. The correct response for anyone after meeting God like this is to say, "If God is holy and just and I am not close to any of those things, then he ought to destroy me."

But God does not punish Jacob. Jacob has nothing; he is nowhere and he has no one. And instead of punishing him, God makes three promises to him, and they are exactly what Jacob needs to hear. First, Jacob has nobody. He is on his own. God says in verse 15, "Behold, I am with you." He is saying, "Jacob, you have nobody. Your mother will never see you again. Your dad does not want to see you again, and you had better hope you never see your brother again. But I am with you." Second, Jacob has nothing. He is penniless. God says in verse 13, "The land on which you lie I will give to you and to your offspring." God is saying, "You have nothing right now, but I am going to give you a nation. I am going to give you a kingdom." Finally, Jacob has no family. Well, he has a family, but they sent him away. God says in verse 14, "Your offspring shall be like the dust of the earth, and you shall spread abroad to the west and to the east and to the north and to the south, and in you and your offspring shall all the families of the earth be blessed." He is saying, "Jacob, you are going to have a wife. You are going to have children. I am going to give you a family." God shows up and says, "You do not have anybody, but I am with you. You do not have anything, but I am going to give you all the wealth you need. You do not have a family, but I am going to give you a family."

Grace is incredibly personal. Jacob knows of God's plan to use his family, but this is the first time he has ever heard from God personally. The Bible is saying, "It does not do any good to be a part of God's plan if you do not know God." Remember that Jacob is a liar, a cheat, and a deceiver, but he is the first guy who ever hears God say, "I am with you."

It is not enough to know about grace conceptually; we have to know about it personally. It is not enough to know that God has a plan. The only way into the story is to experience God's grace personally. When grace comes, it is not just universal; it is personal. In church, we talk often about how grace is God's unmerited favor—we do not deserve it, but he gives it. We say things like "In grace, God forgives the whole world's sins. In grace, God welcomes people into his kingdom. In grace, God loves people." We often forget grace is not just universal but is very personal. Yes, grace does some things for everybody, but it also does something particular for individuals. When God interrupts, when God intercedes, he does not see the individual as yet another person who needs general forgiveness and mercy and grace; rather, he shows up and says, "I know exactly who you are. I have customized my grace." The grace of God is not just universal but is particular in its application.

God shows up. He interrupts and he says to Jacob, "I am going to completely change you, and lest you think I do not know you, here are the three ways you are desperate for change. I am changing all of them." If you are not a Christian and you say, "I could never turn to Jesus because I am too messed up," know that God's grace is not just universal but is particular. God knows you. If Jacob the liar, Jacob the cheater, can be the first guy in all the Bible to hear God say, "I am with you," then how much more can the rest of us hear God say, "I am with you. Not with you in a general sense, but I am with the real you"?

If you are a Christian and you say, "I know that Jesus died for me. I know all this," you do not know if you are not applying that truth particularly. If you are not praying and pleading for God to not just interrupt in your life in a general sense but in a specific sense, you do not know grace—you know *about* grace.

When God shows up and wonderfully interrupts Jacob, he changes Jacob. He brings a personal kind of grace because he is a personal kind of God. God is already the God of Jacob's family, but he is not content with that. He wants to be the God of Jacob. He is saying, "I know what the innermost cry of your heart is. My grace is sufficient to change that." Jacob hears exactly what he needs to hear, and so will you when God interrupts and intercedes into your life specifically. If you are a Christian and there is an area of your life where you are not seeing change, invite him and say, "Please, interrupt me. Bring me a particular kind of grace." If you are not a Christian and you say you could never be a Christian because of certain struggles in your life, please understand that is precisely why we turn to God. Jacob is nowhere, has nothing, is no one, and has nobody. That means he is perfectly ripe for an interruption by God. And that intrusion changes him.

After his dream, Jacob awakes and says, "'Surely the LORD is in this place, and I did not know it.' And he was afraid and said, 'How awesome is this place! This is none other than the house of God, and this is the gate of heaven'" (Genesis 28:16b–17). Jacob is terrified in a wonderful kind of way. The fact that the God of Isaac could show up and bring him personal grace is incredible to him, so he takes the rock that he was sleeping on and he flips it up and pours oil on it, anointing it, and says, "This is going to stand here and be a reminder for everybody that God showed up for me personally, that God is real."

Then, at the end of the chapter, he makes a vow to God. He says, "If it is true that God just interrupted my life, and if it is true that he is on my side even though he should not be, and if it is true that he is going to leverage all that he is for me, not just universally, but personally, then that God is my God." The response of Jacob is to hear what

God said and respond to it by giving himself completely. We know this because he says, "And of all that you give me I will give a full tenth to you" (Genesis 28:22b). God has not even asked for that. Jacob is just giving it; he is saying, "If that is true, then I want to give you everything."

When we encounter God, we do not walk away like we just saw a good movie. We walk away changed. It is not enough to say that God interrupts our lives. We also have to realize that to experience this kind of grace is to be completely and utterly changed. Jacob goes from someone who is self-made, who does not think about consulting God, to saying, "I am not going to trust in my own plans and provision but in your plans and provision. If you lead, then I will follow you." In Genesis 28, we learn that the basis on which we relate to God is this: He makes tremendous promises to us and we believe him. For most of us, our encounter with God reads like a great movie, then we go about our lives, forgetting about it after a short period of time. But if you have met God, if you have personally experienced God, it changes you at your very core. When Jacob sets the rock up and pours oil over it, he is saying, "When I wonder if God is with me, then I will think about this moment."

Jacob's dream means nothing without God being in it. In verse 13, it is important to see that God doesn't stand above the tower but stands above Jacob. All this matters because God himself is speaking with Jacob. He does not send an intermediary; he himself says, "Jacob, I am with you." We cannot really be changed by a personal experience of God's change and an interruption of God unless we meet God. A sermon does not do it; a song does not do it; a Bible study does not do it; a movie does not do it. Only meeting God does it. People will only respond when they meet the living God personally. How will they do that today?

In John 1, Jesus is calling his disciples and he meets Nathanael. John writes, "Jesus saw Nathanael coming toward him and said of him, 'Behold, an Israelite indeed, in whom there is no deceit!' Nathanael said to him, 'How do you know me?' Jesus answered him, 'Before Philip called you, when you were under the fig tree, I saw you.' Nathanael answered him, 'Rabbi, you are the Son of God! You are the King of Israel!' Jesus answered him, 'Because I said to you, "I saw you under the fig tree," do you believe? You will see greater things than these.' And he said to him, 'Truly, truly, I say to you, you will see heaven opened, and the angels of God ascending and descending on the Son of Man'" (John 1:47–51).

Jesus says to Nathanael, "Jacob had a tower on which angels were ascending and descending, and I am that tower. I am the one God has built so he can get to people. I am not a tower people have built to get to God. I am the interruption of grace into this world. Jacob had a dream in the middle of nowhere; I am that dream." Everywhere Jesus goes, he does not have a stock message but a personal message. He says universally, "The problems that you have will be solved only through me," but he applies that statement individually. Jesus is the one who brings us into the experience of God. Everywhere he goes, he restores things. Everywhere he goes, he puts the world back together. Everywhere he goes, he teaches truth as it has never been taught. He lives sinlessly, only to go to the cross, and on the cross when he says, "It is finished," he does not mean that just universally but also personally.

This wonderfully hostile grace is a daily experience for Christians. Jacob could not presume a dream would come from God every day, but we have Jesus, who we can go to every day. We have Jesus, who interrupts and intercedes and intrudes in our lives through the Holy Spirit every day. Guilt says, "You will never be anything." Conviction says, "Because God has interrupted your life, you can be so much more." Do not shy away from this gift of grace. Do not run from it, but lean into it. That is the interruption of God into your life. That is him bringing grace personally. He wants to change your life. He wants to use you. That is God's grace. That is the intrusion God brings into our lives to say he has brought grace not just corporately but personally. Jesus is the true stairway to heaven, and God is coming down to us, interceding and intruding and changing us for his glory and our good.

Chapter 15

Grace That Rescues Us from the Gods

Genesis 29–30:24

Many of us are predisposed to thinking that the Bible is either a book of morals or virtues to which we should adhere, or a book that holds out heroic characters that we should endeavor to be like. One way of bursting these predisposed ideas is to read a large section of Scripture. At the end, you will most likely say, "Boy, if there is a hero in here, I do not know who it is." If you read the story in Genesis 29 and 30, you will see Jacob is not a hero. Leah is not a hero. Rachel is not a hero. Laban is not a hero. There are no heroes. They are just a messed-up family filled with broken people doing the kinds of things that broken people do. We continually need to see that the theme of the Bible is neither a list of morals to which we need to adhere nor the stories of some heroic people we should emulate. Rather, the theme of the Bible is that despite the brokenness of this world, God's sovereign grace is the glue that holds it together and that is bringing about the fruition of God's promises.

In the garden of Eden, Adam and Eve disobey God and eat the fruit they were instructed not to eat. Because of that act, the world is broken, but God promises to send someone to restore the world (Genesis 3:15). God says to Abraham, in Genesis 12 that this someone is going to come from his family. At this juncture, we go from the wide-angle lens of Genesis covering all of humanity, and then we zoom in on the family of Abraham. Abraham eventually has a son named Isaac. Isaac has two sons. God chooses the promise to go to the younger son, Jacob. Jacob gets married twice and has a lot of children, and the story progresses. In spite of the brokenness, in spite of the depravity, in spite of the weakness, God's sovereign grace and the promises he has made continue to march forward.

If you are new to the Bible, if you are thinking through the Bible, or if you grew up in church and you cannot shake the Sunday-school mindset, let passages like this wash over you. Clearly, the Bible is not calling any of us to be like any of these characters. Something else must be going on. That something else is God's sovereign grace. Sovereign because it is not dependent on us, and gracious because we do not deserve it. God is bringing about his promise to send someone to restore the brokenness of the world, and he is doing it through this family that he chose. He chose this family not because this family is the wisest, the best, or the most moral but simply because he is gracious and good.

Since there are no heroes or morals to follow here, another temptation would be to read a passage like this and think, *I have nothing in common with anyone in this passage. These people are so messed up.* That would be a mistake, too. To hold them out as heroes would be a mistake, and to say, "I am nothing like them," would be a mistake. All of us possess a tendency to make much of everybody else's weaknesses and make little of our own. If we read carefully, we can see that these people are actually just like us—and if God's sovereign grace can work in and through them, even though they are messed up, then it can work in and through us.

What Drives Us All

In this story, there are four main characters. They are very different people doing very different things, yet they are all driven by something. All four have something in life that they believe will make them happy and complete. They view the world through this lens because those things they believe will make them happy become the single motivating forces in their lives. Those forces determine their actions and how they see right and wrong.

Laban's single motivation is his desire to be wealthy. He is so motivated by this desire that he is going to do some things that he might not otherwise do. He is going to do them because these decisions will lead toward his ultimate goal of wealth. Many Hebrew scholars argue that the first time Laban meets a member of Abraham's family, it is the servant who comes to get his sister for Isaac to marry and that this servant is passing out gold right and left, so when Laban meets Jacob with hugs and kisses, many Hebrew scholars suggest he is looking for gold. Laban is driven by a desire to be financially secure. If you were to ask him what it takes to be happy or whole or to have purpose, he would say money and financial security.

Jacob is driven by romantic love, or even lust. Jacob shows up and falls in love with Rachel. There's a wonderful verse in which the Bible says he works for seven years but for him it is like a day (Genesis 29:20). At the end of those seven years, he goes to Laban and says, "Give me your daughter." Essentially, he is saying, " ... so I can sleep with her." He is motivated by love and lust. That is why the author tells us that Jacob looks at Rachel and she is beautiful in both form and appearance (Genesis 29:17). In other words, she does not have just a pretty face; she has a good body. Jacob is driven by this one woman; he wants to have this one woman. He is not driven by the desire for a wife in general; he wants this wife. He is not sleeping with any woman; he wants to sleep with this woman. Everything he does is motivated by his desire for this one woman. If you were to ask Jacob what it would take to make him happy, he would say Rachel.

Leah, Jacob's first wife, is driven by a desire for a husband's affection. Everything she does is about getting her husband's affection. She wants to give Jacob children, and when she has them, she names her children in a particular way, trying to turn her husband's head. If you were to ask Leah what it would take to make her happy, she would say she needs her husband to love her; she wants to have a great relationship with her husband.

Rachel is driven by a desire to have children. In the beginning of Chapter 30, she says, "Give me children or I will die." If you were to ask Rachel what life was about, she would say it is about having kids and being a mom.

They are different people doing different things, reacting to situations differently, yet each is driven by one particular thing they have to have. In that way, we are very much like them. All of us have one thing or a few things that we say are going to make us happy, whole, or satisfied. That thing is different for each of us. Some say, "I have to get married." Some say, "I am married, but if life is ever going to be what I want it to be, I have to have a great marriage, like in a movie." Some people will say, "I am married and my marriage is good, but I have to have kids. Life has no meaning without kids." Some people say, "I have to get a job," or "I have to get into a certain industry," or "I have to have this house or this vacation." Whatever drives us, we all believe there is something out there that will make us happy, and we are driven by that thing. They are not all bad things. We do not want to identify with Laban; he is a greedy, opportunistic capitalist. Not everybody in this story is driven by something bad. Leah wants her husband to love her, and that is not a bad thing. Rachel wants children, and that is not a bad thing. Jacob wants to spend his life with the woman he loves, and that is not a bad thing. But they are so driven by these desires that their desires define everything they do. The Bible says that when there is something in our lives that motivates and drives and pushes us, when it becomes the lens through which we see the world, when it becomes the standard by which we determine right or wrong, it becomes a god for us, an idol.

We often think of idols as little statues on mantels that people worship, but idols are not just little statues and they are not limited to greed, children, family, marriage, or romance. Anything can become a god when it becomes the single motivating force in someone's life. When we say no to something or yes to something simply on the basis of whether it helps or hinders us from getting the very thing we want, that thing becomes our god; it becomes what drives us. We all have very different idols. Laban's idol is not Leah's idol, Leah's is not Rachel's, and Rachel's is not Jacob's, but they all have idols.

While they are all looking for different things, it can be argued that they are all looking for love. Laban appears to be looking for money, but he is actually looking for love. Money is, very often, a kind of self-love. When we have money in the bank, we feel secure. No matter what happens, we can pay to fix the problem, but that very security is a form of loving yourself: You want money in the bank so you can love yourself into security. Leah wants her husband to love her. Jacob wants a romantic, passionate relationship. Rachel wants the love of a mom and her children, maternal love. We are all looking for love, and that drives us.

Not every kind of love looks like movie-screen love, but it all comes down to wanting to be valued, celebrated, and loved in the end. It does not matter how our particular desire fleshes out, all of us are driven by the desire to be loved. That desire manifests in a variety of ways, as it did for these four characters, but at the end of the day, we believe if we had a certain type of love from a particular object or person, we would be happy. How do we know what that is for us? Whatever you wake up in the morning thinking about and go to bed at night thinking about, if it tends to be the same thing, that thing is probably your idol.

What Kind of People Do We Become?

When we say, "I have to have that," what kind of people do we become? First, we become people who are violent. We do violence to get the things we want. We see this clearly with Laban. He is not physically violent, but he is emotionally, relationally, and fiscally violent. He is not beating Jacob up, but he is manipulating his daughters and Jacob in an effort to get money. He wants money, so he concocts this whole scheme in his head. Jacob says, "I want to marry your daughter, but I have no job and no real prospects in life. Because I do not have a job or any money, I am going to work for you for seven years. You do not have to pay me. Seven years of free labor will be my payment for your daughter." Laban says yes without committing himself to actually give Rachel to Jacob. Jacob says, "I want to marry Rachel," but Laban says in verse 19, "It is better that I give her [he does not say Rachel's name] to you, than it is I should give to any other man." He never actually says he is going to give up Rachel. He is very sly, and through his deceit, he does violence to Jacob.

But Jacob is not innocent in this situation either. After they go to the ceremony, Jacob is very drunk. At this point, Laban brings Leah to the ceremony, covering everything except the eyes. Jacob is so drunk that when it is time to go to the marriage bed, he does not notice that a woman other than Rachel is brought in. Jacob ends up with another woman.

The next morning, Jacob goes to Laban and says, "What have you done to me?" Laban replies, "Here, we never do anything for the younger before we do it for the firstborn." He is saying, "Jacob, I simply did the same thing to you that you did to your dad" (see Genesis 27:1–40 for context). Jacob has been deceived, just as he deceived his father. Jacob is not innocent; he has done violence, and Laban is saying, "I knew what I wanted, and I did violence to get it, just like you did."

Laban and Jacob are not the only ones that are violent, however. The women are violent too. In fact, Leah and Rachel both do to Jacob what Sarah did to Abraham: They give their servants to their husbands and say, "Sleep with our servants and get those women pregnant." Then when those women get pregnant, they take those children and keep them for themselves. We can say, "Well, that was the culture back then," but simply because something is culturally acceptable does not mean it is victimless. These women are taking their servants' children as if some sort of child arms race is going on here. There is incredible violence happening.

In addition to participating in the race for children, Rachel possesses another type of violence. It is not just violence to others; it is an existential violence. Look at what Rachel says in Genesis 30:1: "Give me children or I shall die." When we say, "I have to have this," we will ultimately get violent with ourselves. Jacob loves Rachel, not Leah, but Leah keeps popping out babies, hoping Jacob will love her. In Genesis 30, he is still sleeping with Rachel; he is not sleeping with Leah. That is why Rachel offers Leah a chance to sleep with Jacob in return for mandrakes. Jacob is Rachel's to give because Jacob loves Rachel, even without children. So who is putting pressure on Rachel to have children? Rachel is. She is saying life is not worth living if she does not have kids. When you say, "I will only be happy if I have _____," you will step on people to get that thing you think will produce happiness, but you will also do violence to yourself. Some of us work so hard because we are afraid of having to look ourselves in the mirror if we are not successful. Some of us have to get married because we feel like we are completely hideous or we are unworthy or some kind of freak if we do not get married. That is existential violence to ourselves.

Finally, Rachel also does violence to Jacob. She says, "Give me children, or I will die." Jacob asks, "Am I God?" Jacob is saying, "I am trying, but I am not God. I cannot do that." So many marriages break under the weight of this kind of violence. Someone somewhere says, "I will never be happy unless I am married. I have never been happy, but if I got married, I would be happy," so they get married and essentially say to their spouse, "My whole life, I have not been able to be happy. I need you to make me happy in one day." Eventually, the marriage implodes because one person is doing emotional violence to the other spouse by saying, "Your job is to make me completely and utterly happy." The other is saying (without saying it), "Am I God? How do I make you happy all the time?"

When we have one thing we want, we do all kinds of violence to others including those we care about, but violence is not the only thing we do. We also become victims. We not only dish out violence but receive violence. Jacob is a victim. Laban will be a victim when his daughters eventually leave him, take all his stuff, and completely disown him. Leah is a victim. Rachel is a victim. How did it get to the point where she says, "If I do not have kids, I would rather die"? She is a victim of the culture and of herself. In Genesis 29:31, when Leah begins to have children, she has a son and she names him Reuben, which literally means "He sees." She basically says, "Now that I have a son, my husband will see me." Jacob does not see her, however, so she has another son named, literally, "He hears." She is saying, "Now that I have another son, maybe Jacob will hear me." Then she has another son, and she names him "attached," meaning, "Maybe now my husband and I will really be attached." There is pain in this process, until finally, she hires Jacob with some mandrakes and has another son she names Issachar, meaning "I paid him wages." Look at the path from desire to desperation to victimization: "He will see me"; "He will hear me"; "We will be attached"; and finally, "I had to pay to sleep with him."

In the church, this type of idolatry happens continually. We have said, "Do not party," and "Do not live for money." We have told people instead "Live for family. Have the perfect family and the perfect house and the perfect kids and the white picket fence." And the people who cannot have children or cannot get married, or who have all of that but are not happy, feel utterly crushed by a church that has turned them into victims. It does not matter if what you desire is a good thing or a bad thing, if you chase it and make it the one thing you have to have, it will crush you and you will crush yourself.

When Jacob awakes from his marriage night, the author writes, "In the morning, behold, it was Leah." Derek Kidner, an Old Testament scholar, says that in this one verse, you have the whole human condition. Every time we think we have a Rachel, we go to bed with it. When we wake up, we find it is Leah. Every time we say, "This job will make me happy," we get that job and we wake up in the morning and are not happy. The job is like waking up to Leah. Every time we say, "This boyfriend or girlfriend," or "this marriage and this kid," or "this job and these possessions. These will make me happy," we go to bed with it and we wake up with Leah. We become victims of our own desires and plans.

Not only will we do violence, not only will we become victims, but we also will become spiritually vacant. Where is God in this passage? He is there in every third or fourth sentence. He is doing things people do not even know. People are not acknowledging him. Rachel wants to have kids, but she is not going to God; she grabs her servant. Jacob wants Rachel, but he does not go to God; he crafts a plan to work for seven years and get her. Leah wants to turn her husband's heart toward her. She does not pray; she starts popping out babies. There is a spiritual vacuum here. Even beyond that, people begin to attribute things to God that are not God's doing. The women give their servants to their husband, and he sleeps with the servants and then the servants have kids. The wives say, "Oh, God gave me children!" as if, way back in Genesis 2, God created Adam, Eve, and Eve's assistant. In Genesis 2 when the world was perfect, there was not Adam and Eve and Jill and Susan; it was just Adam and Eve.

This scheming is clearly outside of God's plan, but this is what happens. When we build our lives around other gods, when we say, "God is not ultimate; children are ultimate," or "God is not ultimate; my career is ultimate," we do great violence to God. If God is not better than our kids, then he is not really that great. If God is not better than being married, then he is not really that great. When we say, "I live for marriage. I live for kids. I live for work," we are reducing God and doing violence to God. Essentially, we are saying there is no God.

If everybody gets to pick the thing worth living for, if everybody gets to say, "This is what life is about," then we are all manufacturing God. If we are all manufacturing God, then there is no God and we create a spiritual vacuum, a vacancy. If you are willing to say there is one thing you are living for, can you agree that all three of these things are true?

1. You have done great violence to get this one thing .

2. You feel victimized when things don't turn out as you expected.

3. You are left spiritually vacant.

We look for love in all of the wrong things, and in the morning, they are always Leah.

How We Might Escape

If all this is true, how do we escape it? We don't see much escape in these two chapters of Genesis. All these characters go on to chase the things they think will satisfy them. They hurt each other. They destroy each other. Even their sons will go on to hurt each other; it is generational. But there is a brief glimpse of hope at the end of Genesis 29. Leah keeps having children, saying, "Now he sees me. Now he hears me. Now we will be attached. I had to pay for this." Then she has a fifth son, named Judah, which means "praise." Genesis 29:35 says, "And she conceived again and bore a son and said, 'This time I will praise the LORD.' Therefore, she called his name Judah and she ceased bearing." She gets a brief window into something that will break this cycle. This something will keep her from needing Jacob's love, even if she still wants it. It will keep her from doing violence, keep her from being a victim, and keep her from being spiritually vacant. She realizes the love she has been seeking from her husband is ultimately to be found in God. She says, "This time, I will praise the LORD." In doing so, she uses the name Yahweh, the covenant name of God. She does not use the generic Hebrew word for god. She says, "This time, I will praise the personal God of this family who has made himself known to us and has shown love to me." In verse 31, the author writes, "When the LORD saw Leah was hated, he opened her womb." God sees her and loves her, and she becomes convinced of that.

In a brief moment, Leah says, "If God's love for me is true, I do not need Jacob to hear me, see me, or be attached to me. I want it, but I do not need it if I have God." The way to escape the cycle of violence and victimization is to know God in such a personal way that we do not need anything. We can want things in the world, but we do not need. We are satisfied in knowing God loves us personally.

The son Leah has when she comes to the realization that God loves her is Judah. In Genesis 3, God says he is going to send someone and that someone is going to restore the world. He speaks to Abraham and says that someone is going to come from his family. Abraham has Isaac, and God says the promise is going to flow through Isaac. Isaac has Jacob and Esau, and God says it is going to be Jacob, who is the promise bearer. From these twelve sons of Jacob, the promise bearer of this family will be Judah. We go from Abraham to Isaac, from Isaac to Jacob, from Jacob to Judah, and from Judah on and on until we get all the way to the Gospel of Matthew, where the promise ends with Jesus. Jesus is the walking and talking expression of God's love. God says to Leah, "You do not need Jacob's love; you have mine," and she understands for a second. She understands it enough to give her kid a name of praise. She does go right back to mandrakes and manipulation, but for a moment, she gets it.

Jesus embodies that praise of Leah. When Jesus came, he said, "I have come not to be served, but to serve and give my life as a ransom for many" (Mark 10:45). Here, Jesus is saying that he is driven and that what drives him is the desire to love people. He is the tangible expression of God's love to people. He is not driven to get love; he is driven to give it. He is so driven to love, that drive takes him to the cross, where he undergoes violence. When we are driven, we will do great violence. This is also true of God. He is so driven to rescue sinners, he does great violence, but in God's sovereign grace, he is doing violence to himself. On the cross, God is both the perpetrator of violence and the victim of violence at the same time. When Jesus is on the cross, he says, "My God! My God! Why have you forsaken me?" (Matthew 27:46b). He becomes spiritually vacant in our place. On the cross, God the Father is saying, "Because you are violent and spiritually vacant, you deserve for me to judge you," but on the cross, God the Son is saying, "I am so driven to rescue God's people that I will undergo the violence. I will become a victim in your place. I will enter into your spiritual vacancy so you might know my spiritual relationship with God."

If you are not a Christian, the only way to break free from the cycle of need and violence is to see God entered into this violence for you. While you are driven by a job, he is driven by love for you. While you are driven by a desire for sex, he is driven by a desire to build God's kingdom, including you. You are driven to look for love in all the wrong places, but God became flesh, driven to show you love in the right place, by becoming a victim of his own violence, entering into your spiritual vacancy. He then rose from the dead to say, "Now you can know that the love you are looking for is found in me." The beginning point of seeking Jesus is understanding that living for sex does not work, living for marriage does not work, living for children does not work, and living for a job does not work. We are meant to find our fulfillment in God.

If you are a Christian, do not run headlong right back into the cycle of violence and victimization. So many of us claim Jesus as the source of our satisfaction but live for work, for kids, or for marriage. We say we love Jesus, then we find good things and live for them. We think our lives are not idolatrous because children are great and careers are great. They may be great, but they are not God. A good work ethic is great, but it is not God. A good marriage is great, but it is not God. There is a big difference between wanting and needing. The Gospel says we can want things, but we have been set free from needing those very same things that used to enslave us. We do not have to do violence to get those things to love us, because at the end of the day, if we cannot get them, we do not need them, because we have God's love. We do not have to be victimized or say things like "If I do not have children, I am going to die," because though we may not have children and we want them, and even though we are heartbroken by it, we have God.

The Gospel comes to us and says we have all we need in the love of God shown to us in the life, death, and resurrection of Jesus. We can want these other things because God is a good God and often gives those things—but for some of us, for God to give us the things we are looking for would be the worst possible thing he could do. Those who know Jesus cannot be driven by the same cycles of desire, violence, and victimization as those who do not. We are those who stand outside the cycle and say there is grace that rescues us from the gods—the sovereign grace of God shown to us in the life, death, and resurrection of Jesus Christ.

Chapter 16

A Grace That Wonderfully Wounds

Genesis 32:22–32

When God sees fit to repeat himself in the Bible, we would do well to join him in this repetition through the studying of his word. God's word is like a diamond: We can turn it and there is always a new angle. As we walk through Genesis, we are not inventing new principles on grace, but we are looking at how this grace comes to different people. God's sovereign grace comes to different people, but it is not always the same, and that is good for us. Some of us can identify with Abraham but not Sarah. Some of us can identify with the loneliness and bitterness of Sarah, but not Jacob. Some of us can identify with Jacob, who is scheming and manipulative and self-sufficient, but not the other two. God displays his sovereign grace through a variety of individuals. Through this, he shows us that his sovereign grace is the hope of not just one people or even one group of people. His grace is the hope of all people over all time, and it comes to us irrespective of our personality, situation, time, or place.

When Grace Comes to Us

Genesis 32:24 says, "Jacob was left alone." Grace comes to us when we are alone. Specifically, experiencing God's grace is an individual experience. At this point in Jacob's life, he is around the story of God, although you might debate whether he is in it. He has four wives, a big family, and lots of possessions. His life is great in some ways and is a mess in other ways; it is filled with noise. But he experiences grace in a way that changes him when he is left alone. We all experience grace when we are alone. It is very easy to get swept up in the momentum of a movement but to miss the fact that you do not have an individual experience of God's grace. Short of having an individual experience with the God of grace, no one is a part of God's plan or purpose or movement or people. If we look back to Genesis 12, we see that God speaks to Abraham individually. Later, in Genesis 18, he comes and speaks to Sarah individually. In Genesis 26, God speaks to Isaac individually, and here, he comes to Jacob alone.

Whatever kind of background you come from, unless you have met God in his grace alone, you have not met him at all. Many of us have a familial faith or a social faith but do not actually have an individual faith. Alfred North Whitehead, a professor of philosophy at Harvard in the beginning of the twentieth century, said, "Religion is what a man does with his solitariness." It is a great way of saying that if you want to know if you really know God, you cannot find out when you are around other people and music is playing and hands are up and eyes are closed. Religion is not about getting caught up in the emotion. It is not about getting caught up in the movement. It is to answer the following question: When you are alone, is God with you?

Before this encounter, Jacob is around the story and near the story of God's sovereign grace. He is very close to what God is doing, but God is going to show up when he is alone and say, "You do not know me, Jacob. You are not with me. You are around what I am doing, but you are not with me; I am not with you. We are not together." Heaven is full of people from every tribe, tongue, and nation with different lives and different experiences, but the one thing they have in common is that each had an individual experience with God.

This does not mean when we experience God's grace, we have to be physically alone. If that were the case, today, none of us could experience God's grace, because there are a lot of people around us all the time and we are seldom alone. It is possible to meet God in a crowded room, but unless you meet him individually in that room, you do not know him. Have you ever wondered why you feel very close to God on Sunday mornings, but come Monday or Tuesday, you do not? It is because, as Alfred North Whitehead said, you do not really have religion, because religion is what happens when you are alone. When we continually attend church services, we run the risk of chasing the high—we are admitting that when we are alone, we do not have God. But when we do not know God individually, we do not know him at all.

God has orchestrated the circumstances of Jacob's life through his love and sovereignty so Jacob will be alone for this encounter. In Genesis 12, God says to Abraham, "I am going to make the world new and I am going to do it through your family." Abraham has a wife, Sarah, and they keep getting older and think God's promise is never going to happen, but it does when they have their son, Isaac. They have Isaac, and God promises to make the world new through Isaac's family. Isaac has two children—Jacob and Esau. Esau is the older, and the promise should go to him because he is the firstborn, but God says, "No, I do not choose Esau. I choose Jacob" (Genesis 25:19–26), so the promise moves forward with Jacob, who cheats and manipulates his older brother (Genesis 25:29–34, 27:1–40). Esau plots to kill him, so Jacob goes into hiding. In the passage we are studying, Jacob is back, but the situation is not resolved. Jacob is getting ready to cross the river to his homeland, but he knows that Esau is coming his way with 400 armed men.

As we know, Jacob is very smart and manipulative. He takes all he has and sends it in waves to his brother. Every time a new wave of people and items comes to meet Esau, the people are supposed to tell him, "This is a gift for Esau from Jacob." Jacob's hope is that by the time

Esau actually gets to Jacob, Esau will have lots of stuff and be happy. That is the plan, but Jacob is not sure it is going to work, so he moves his family across the river. This way, if Esau attacks and kills him, maybe Jacob's family can get away. Jacob is completely and utterly alone, and that is exactly where he needs to be.

Have you ever been in a situation where things go so completely south for you, you realize how completely alone and how much of an individual you really are? Martin Lloyd Jones, a famous British preacher, said it like this: "You are going to go to the hospital and you are going to have surgery, and when you are in the waiting room, your family is around you saying, 'We are here for you. We are in this together,' but when the doctor comes to get you and says, 'It is time,' they all go to lunch. You are not actually in this together." As they are wheeling you into the operating room, you realize how utterly and completely alone you are. Alone is exactly where God wants us. When we are alone, we ask, "God, where are you?" When we have everything and we do not feel alone, we are not praying.

If God did not bring us to a place where we realize how truly alone we are, we would not seek him. We would not know we needed him. Jacob at every point in his life has been completely self-sufficient. He schemes and he manipulates. He finds a way to cheat his brother and father; he finds a way to get the woman he wants; he finds a way to get rich by cheating his father-in-law, and now he thinks he has found a way to buy his way out of the doom that awaits once he crosses the river. He has manipulated his way through everything, but God strategically positions him so he will understand that he is completely alone, and God says to him, "Yes, you are alone, Jacob. It does not matter what else is going on. It is about you and me."

Some of us feel so completely alone that we are tempted to lash out at God. But God, in his grace, has a way of bringing us to this place where we say, "I am alone, God. Where are you?" And God says, "Now we can do this. Now we can talk. Now I can show you grace." The reality is that we live in a culture where we are seldom alone. We have continuous noise around us. Some of us work eighty hours a week because we do not want to be alone. We do not want the lack of noise to culminate in an existential understanding that we are individuals and that, no matter who is around us, we are alone. God says that is precisely where we need to be. Oftentimes, when it feels like God is trying to kill us, he is actually loving us more. Jacob could ask, "God, if you are real, why am I giving everything away, trying to save my life? Why have I had to send my wife and children away? Why am I giving everything away to try to save my life? If you are real, then where are you?" But if we go back and read the previous four or five chapters dealing with Jacob, we will find that the one thing he never does is pray. As long as Jacob can see a way out, he does not look for God. It is when he cannot see a way out that he actually meets God.

The most loving thing God can do for some of us is bring us to a point where we know there is absolutely nothing we can do. When we come to this point, he has our attention and he can finally speak to us. There is going to be a time in our lives when our health leaves us and we ask, "God, where are you?" There are going to be times when our relationships crumble and we ask, "God, where are you?" There are going to be times when our careers fall apart and we ask, "God, where are you?" Every one of those times, God will say, "Finally. You are looking for me." Meeting with God has to be individual, and God will providentially work through our circumstances to get us alone. It is not because he hates us or is trying to kill us. It is because he loves us. If we are honest with ourselves, we admit we only seek God when we are alone. He knows that, too.

How Grace Comes to Us

When grace comes, it comes violently. The weaving together of grace and violence is a very foreign concept to us. When we think about grace, we think of the mercy of a grandpa god with candy who wants to tell us we are all loved. We think of hugs and warm fuzzies. In Jacob's life, there are no hugs or pillows with nice sayings stitched into the fabric. There is a great violence because grace is violent for Jacob. It is not comforting, soft, or cuddly.

Grace is a violent interruption to Jacob, the one who always has a plan. He is heading back to the promised land, and he is going to get what is rightfully his. He is going to live in the land and have descendants like the sand on the shore and the stars in the sky. All these promises are going to be his, but there is an obstacle to that plan. That obstacle is Esau, so Jacob concocts a plan to placate his brother and to reconcile through his schemes and manipulations. When God shows up, he interrupts this plan. He begins to wrestle Jacob. It is a violent intrusion. History is full of people who would say, "I was going a certain way and then I met God and he violently interrupted my life, so I ended up going a different way. Even though I like going this new way now, change was a violent intrusion into my life." This happens throughout the Bible. The Apostle Paul, then named Saul, was traveling to Damascus to persecute Christians. When he met God on his way to the city, he was struck blind and violently turned in the other direction, to where he actually helped found several New Testament churches (Acts 9). All over the Bible, God is showing up, interrupting, and saying, "I know you think you are doing this and going here, but you are not. We are doing something new now." Grace is a violent interruption.

Grace is also a violent contradiction. God shows up and they wrestle. This seems weird, but in this culture, wrestling was a way to resolve legal disputes. If you lost the wrestling match, then you lost everything for which you were wrestling. One commentator says wrestling is contradiction. When the person you are wrestling wants to go this way, you pull them back in. When they push, you pull. When they zig, you zag. God shows up and he is contradicting Jacob, but the match is not just physical; it is metaphysical. Jacob believes everything in his life will make sense if he can resolve things with Esau. He believes the key to a happy life is Esau not killing him. He has leveraged all that he can because he thinks the biggest enemy in his life is Esau. God shows up to contradict all this. He says, "Your biggest enemy is not Esau; it is me.

Your biggest obstacle is not Esau; it is me. You have always thought that by wrestling with someone, you could be happy. You struggled with your brother since the day you were born and thought it would bring you happiness. Then you struggled with your father and you thought that would make you happy. Then you struggled with your father-in-law and you thought if you won his possessions, you would be happy. Now you think if you appease your brother, you will be happy. But you are not really wrestling them; you are wrestling me. Your problem is that you fundamentally think you can manipulate any situation to your advantage. You are looking inwardly, when you ought to be looking spiritually." They are not just wrestling; God is contradicting the very core of Jacob's being.

God wrestles with Jacob all night as a metaphor symbolizing the struggle of Jacob's life. The two are really wrestling, but the wrestling is a metaphor. God interrupts Jacob, contradicts him, and confronts him. God eventually breaks Jacob. He touches him once around daybreak, and Jacob falls apart. At the end, he is clinging to God, saying, "I will not let you go unless you bless me." God asks him, "What is your name?" and he replies, "Jacob." When we read that, we do not think it is a big deal, but in that culture, your name was everything. Names stood for something. Whatever your name meant was the overarching umbrella for your identity. "Jacob" literally means "deceiver" or "cheater," so when God asks, "What is your name?" he is not simply asking, "What is your name?" He is asking, "Do you know who you are?"

Grace is undeserved favor. It is a beautiful concept, but you can never embrace its truth until you embrace the undeserved part. That is the underbelly of grace that nobody ever talks about. We all sing, "Amazing grace, how sweet the sound that saved a wretch like me." For that to mean anything, we have to say, "I am a wretch." That is what God is doing when he is confronting Jacob. He is saying, "I know exactly who you are. Do you? Are you willing to admit this really is your fault? You deserve to die. You deserve your brother to kill you. Do you know that?"

Why do we need to know that God's grace violently interrupts, violently contradicts, and violently confronts? In our culture, we are told from the time we are little kids that we are snowflakes, unique in every way. As we grow up, we are told we can be whatever we want to be, we just have to set goals and have dreams and that is what life is about. As we set out to accomplish these dreams, we surround ourselves with people who believe in us and we get rid of the people who do not. And so we reach for the stars. When we start to look for God after a life of these pursuits and beliefs, we look for a god that will play the part of accessory. We are saying, "God, I want to do this with my life. Insomuch as you are going to come along beside me and support my plans, goal, and vision, great." We know we do this if we look at how we pray. Most of us pray, "God, I really need to do well. God, I really want to do well on this test. God, I really want to get into this program. God, I really need this big break at work. God, I really need a wife. God, I really need a husband." When we pray like this, we are really saying, "God, I need you to serve my goals. I want you to serve my vision." We then get angry with God when he does not do what we think he is supposed to do while in our service.

When God shows up to Jacob, he is not interested in Jacob's plan or vision. He does not show up and say, "Jacob, I wanted to wrestle, but I know you are a snowflake and snowflakes are very delicate." Instead, he violently interrupts. He violently confronts. He violently changes Jacob. He contradicts Jacob. Some of us have no room for a god who will contradict us. If our god never contradicts or challenges us, we are not looking for God; we want to be God. If we are really in a relationship with someone, on any level, they interrupt us, contradict us, and confront us. Take marriage for example. Marriage has been described as two selfish people colliding. The rest of our lives are wreckage. Your spouse knows you, and when you need it, they contradict you. That is real love. If we never confronted each other, it would mean we are not in love but are pretending, either ignoring what is there or not caring enough to do any real work. If that is true of all our human relationships, how much more so is it true of our relationship with God? Do we really think Almighty God is interested in showing up and being our concierge? Do we really think he exists to serve our vision, plan, and purpose, or do we see that when God shows up, he has to confront us, contradict us, and change us?

When we become unsettled and changing, we can know we are beginning to meet God. Abram becomes Abraham. Sarai becomes Sarah. Jacob becomes Israel. God changes people, but he does so through a violent process. Any Christian throughout history who has done anything in their faith will say when they met God, it was incredibly violent; we are being ripped out of who we used to be and being made into something new. We should not shy away from that process but embrace it. It is love. Every time God shows up, there is wrestling. There is struggle and conflict. We are hard-wired to think that any time God shows up and challenges us, he does not love us. The opposite is true.

God challenging him is exactly what Jacob needs. He has been scheming and manipulating his whole life. He thinks he is self-sufficient. How does God get through to a self-sufficient, arrogant man? He has to attack him. The biggest enemy of grace is not evil; it is self-sufficiency. As long as we think we can look inward for answers, we will never turn to God, but when God wonderfully attacks us, he has what it takes to get through to us. All of us think if God dropped down right now and said, "Here is what I want you to do," we would say, "Okay, God." That is not the case. He must wrestle with us. We need to stop thinking God is trying to kill us and start thinking he is loving us and we are just that hard-hearted and hard-headed.

Where Grace Leads Us

When God gets us alone and violently interrupts, he is trying to take us to weakness. The author writes in verse 25, "When the man saw that he did not prevail over Jacob, he touched his hip socket. And Jacob's hip was put out of joint as he wrestled with him." We read this narrative and we think this wrestling match is an epic struggle and

God is struggling to beat Jacob, but that is not true. God wrestles with Jacob all night to show Jacob that Jacob thinks he can beat God. In the end, God barely touches Jacob and Jacob's hip breaks. If God had just shown up and blown out Jacob's hip without the wrestling, Jacob would not have understood. God gets Jacob to a point of weakness. He touches Jacob's hip, and the man's whole leg falls apart. Jacob will limp for the rest of his life.

The Bible teaches that if anyone were to see God the Father face-to-face, that person would die. Jacob knows that, because later on, in verse 30, he says, "I have seen God face-to-face, yet I did not die." Jacob has gone from wrestling with God like a man to wrestling with God like a child. He has his arms around God's ankle, saying, "I will not let you go until you bless me." He is weak. He is not presuming or arguing. He grabs onto God, and in his weakness, he realizes that for his whole life, he has thought all these other things would make him happy, but they are all worthless. If he has God alone, he is happy.

Jacob could not get to this realization without violence. He could not get there because as long as he was strong, he was not looking for God—but in his weakness, he is clinging to God's ankle, saying, "I am not letting you go until I know you are on my side." He needs to know that God is bigger than him in order to reach for God. The only way for Jacob to know that God is bigger than him is for God to show him through gracious, violent force. We live in a culture where weakness is never a virtue and strength is always good. We hate being weak. We are driven to succeed primarily because we do not want to be weak. The Bible flips all of that on its head and says true strength is found in weakness. It is in weakness that we stop trying to wrestle God and start clinging to his ankle, asking for him alone. God gets Jacob by breaking him. God says, "Your name shall no longer be Jacob; but Israel, for you have striven with God and with men and have prevailed" (Genesis 32:28). That is an interesting way to win. Jacob wins by becoming weak and reaching for God, but God also becomes weak for him.

Verse 25 says, "The man saw that he did not prevail against Jacob." This man is God. What does it mean that the man did not prevail? He does not destroy Jacob because he does not want to destroy Jacob. God becomes weak and restrains himself in order to get through to Jacob. We are prone to ask, "Why does God wrestle Jacob? Why does he hurt his hip? That is not a very Godlike thing to do, is it?" But there are deeper questions than these. You know you are getting close to the person of God when you ask, "Why does God wrestle with Jacob and not completely and utterly annihilate him? Why does God wrestle with Jacob and not break his leg and make him sit on his knees until Esau comes to exact his revenge?" But none of that happens.

God touches Jacob on the sinew of the thigh. In Genesis 24, Abraham sent his servant to find a wife for Isaac. He had this servant swear an oath by making him put his hand under Abraham's thigh. The thigh is really a euphemism for his genitals, which represents that he was making a deal with his servant. This action says, "Judgment will come to my own descendants if I break this promise." Abraham is saying, "I am swearing to you by my offspring." God touches Jacob on the thigh in a similar manner. God does not destroy Jacob but wounds him in the thigh because he is pointing us forward to one of Jacob's descendants, Jesus Christ, who will not only be wounded by God but destroyed by God. God does not destroy Jacob for his sin because he knows that centuries later, God is going to destroy his own sinless son, Jesus. When Jesus is in the garden, asking if there is any other way, God says there is no other way, so Jesus sets his face forward on the glory and joy of obeying God (Matthew 26:36–46). Jesus goes to the cross, paying for the sins of Jacob.

Jacob's problem is not that Esau is coming in judgment. His problem is that one day, God will. God fixes that problem by sending someone from Jacob's thigh—Jesus. Jesus is not just wounded in the thigh but is broken for us, abused for us, killed for us. You know you are beginning to understand the gospel when you say, "If I open myself up to God, how do I know that I will not be destroyed? How do I know

God will not break my life and leave me in pieces? How do I know God will not wound me and leave me limping?" You know because you look to the one who comes from Jacob's lineage. You look at Jesus. Three days after God the Father killed God the Son for our sins, he raised God the Son from the dead. With the resurrection, God is saying, "What I break, I build back up. What I kill, I raise back up. What I destroy, I put back together." He is offering through Jesus an opportunity to open ourselves up to him. If we let him violently interrupt us and make us weak, we have an opportunity to run to Jesus and say, "My only hope is that, like Jacob, I should be destroyed. But Jesus Christ's body was destroyed and his blood was spilled for me." If we run to Christ, God will not just break us down; he will build us up.

That is the beauty of the Gospel. We get to put ourselves in God's hands. We can pray terrifying prayers like "God, do whatever it takes to get ahold of me. Do whatever it takes to get my attention. Do whatever it takes to get through to me. If that is a zero balance, fine. If that is a hospital bed, fine. If that is a life of singleness, fine. If that is a life of physical pain, fine. Because I know whatever you break, you will build back up. You will restore."

If you are not a Christian, this is the Gospel. The Gospel is understanding that you and I are so hard-hearted and arrogant that we will never know that we need him unless he confronts us and weakens us. We will march headlong into his judgment. God weakens us because he loves us. Now we can cling to his ankle and say, "I do not have any right to ask this, but how do I get you?" And when we do, God the Father will point us to the cross and say, "Because Christ was broken, because Christ rose from the dead, you can have me." In these passages, Jacob does not actually see God's face, but one day, we will. Today, we see God in the person of Jesus. In the future, we will see God's face on the day when he reconciles the Church to himself finally and eternally. Do not shy away from God when God breaks you. You need to be broken. We have to be broken, but in the rubble, we can look to Jesus. We will be broken but resurrected with him.

Christian, you are being made new, but the process of making you anew is a violent process of interrupting, confronting, and contradicting. God does this because he loves you. It feels like he does not love you because you are resisting. Throw yourself on the mercy of God. What God breaks, he fixes. What God destroys, he builds back up.

Chapter 17

A Life Shaped by Sovereign Grace: Grace That Goes before Us

Genesis 37:2–36

No matter what subject you are studying at school or even in church, there comes a point when the student says, "So what? What difference does this make in real life?" Moses understood this when he was putting Genesis together, so he ended the book with an application using the life of Joseph. Joseph is a living, breathing lesson on what it looks like to live under God's grace. We're going to look at Joseph as an example of a guy who lives under God's sovereign grace, and flesh out what that looks like in his life.

In Joseph's life, we have a 30,000-foot aerial view of what it looks like to live under God's sovereign grace. We will see that Joseph'es his family and he rescues all of Egypt from famine. Joseph is a person who accomplishes great things.

Perhaps most fascinating about Joseph is his treatment of his brothers in Genesis 50:20. Joseph says to his brothers, the very brothers who did monstrous things to him, "What you meant for evil, God meant for good, in order that He might bring about His purposes and rescue people." Joseph's significance is not that he rises to political power. It is not that he rescues a people. It is not that he has a great job and he is the envy of everybody. Rather, it is that at the end of his life, despite all that he has gone through, he says, "Hey, everything in my life that other people meant for evil, God meant for good."

The very things that, at the time, felt like they were going to crush him, Joseph saw as God doing something good in his life. That's a fascinating perspective to take on life. We are all people who have had our lives crushed, will have our lives crushed, or are even now having our lives crushed by the evil of others, by the evil that we do, and by painful circumstances. Is it possible to come to the point where we would say, "All of these things that have happened were not for my bad but for my good"? If we want that kind of perspective, we have to understand how Joseph gets to that perspective.

What Joseph Is Born Into

Joseph is the son of Jacob, and as we've discovered, Jacob was not the greatest guy in the world. Jacob's family was torn apart through favoritism and partiality, and Joseph is born into a similarly dysfunctional, broken family, filled with rivalry and factions. Joseph becomes the object of his father's affection. In fact, Jacob loves Joseph so much more than the other boys that everybody knows it! Verse 4 says, "But when his brothers saw that their father loved him more than all his brothers, they hated [Joseph], and could not speak peacefully to him." Jacob is not even slick with his favoritism. He buys Joseph a very intricate coat that Joseph could have only because his family is so wealthy that work is optional. This is not a work coat, and it is certainly not something to be worn casually. And every time Joseph wears it, his brothers get more angry. For Joseph, the coat is a sign of his father's love. For Joseph's brothers, it is a sign of their father's favoritism. This is the environment in which Joseph is born and raised. Like all of us, he did not have an opportunity to handpick his family.

Some of what happens to Joseph has nothing to do with him but is caused by circumstances beyond his control. He was born to the wrong family, at the wrong time, and in the wrong social environment. It almost did not matter what he said or did, he was going to be hated. Many people struggle through difficult circumstances by no fault of their own. When you are that person, you have that feeling that you are born unlucky. You can't seem to get healthy or catch a break. You were born into a destructive family or a difficult economic situation. You just can't seem to get ahead, and every time you try, you just can't rise above because circumstances are always against you. It is very tempting in those moments to say, "If God is in charge, he is unfair. Why does that person over there have all these things and I don't have anything? Why are they married, with children, and I can't even get a girl to return my call? Why is that person flying up the career ladder but I can't even figure out what I want to do? Why are circumstances always against me? Why doesn't God care about me?"

The guy who is going to say, "All the evil in my life, God brought about for good," is the same guy who was born into these difficult circumstances. Those same circumstances are ultimately going to be God's means of getting Joseph where God wants him. Joseph could lob the same accusations at God that we do, times ten—and if we continue in our accusations, we will get the understanding that God is only the god of people who have perfect normal lives, that God is the god only of the people for whom things always seem to go right. A lot of preaching that is popular today will profess that the way you know God loves you is if everything breaks right, and yet Joseph, who believes that any evil perpetrated against him is a means for God to display his goodness, was born into and lived through very difficult circumstances. God is also the God of people born under unlucky stars and into difficult circumstances.

What Joseph Steps Into

Lest we make Joseph only into the victim, we need to understand the problems of his life are not just the ones Joseph is born into. It's also the ones he steps into. There is a danger in us saying, "Oh, poor Joseph!" Most modern representations of Joseph depict him as an innocent victim swept up in a grand familial controversy, but that's actually not the whole truth. If we look at the very beginning of the passage, we will see that Joseph brings a bad report regarding his brothers to their father. In the original language, this report means that, at best, Joseph has manipulated the facts to present his brothers in the worst possible light. At worst, it means he has outright lied about them. When you are the most loved son, the worst possible thing would be to lose that status, so in order to solidify his position, Joseph goes to his dad and says, "You know what, Dad? I've got something to tell you about my brothers. Look at what they did. ... You're not going to believe what they said. ... You're not going to believe what they did with your shepherding business and what they're doing with your money." Jacob gets angry with the other sons, and the brothers get angry with Joseph. Joseph is a liar, but he's not just a liar, he's incredibly narcissistic!

It is easy to see the connection between what Joseph is born into and what Joseph steps into. If your father told you that you were the best, if he gave you the best garment imaginable, and if he spent all his time with you at the expense of your siblings, it would be hard not to be narcissistic. Joseph is the golden child, and he enjoys being the golden child. He even comes to his family and talks about some dreams that he had. Today, we all assume the dreams came from God because they somehow, in some way, come true; however, most Hebrew scholars say Joseph's dreams are the only dreams in all of Genesis that have no mention of anything God said. When Abraham dreamed, God spoke. When Abimelech dreamed, God spoke. Here, there's no mention of God.

Robert Alter, a world-renowned Hebrew expert, says he thinks these dreams are blasphemous. In Joseph's last dream, even the stars in the heavens are bowing down to him (Genesis 37:9). Another commentator, Gerhard von Rad, says that "these are the narcissistic dreams of an arrogant, spoiled brat." Even if these dreams are from God, which is debatable, what kind of an arrogant guy do you have to be to walk into a room full of people who hate you, and say, "Hey, let's compare sheaves"?

What kind of a guy does that? A narcissist. To top it off, because apparently his brothers' reaction is not enough, Joseph goes to his dad and says, "Dad, you were in my dream and you were bowing down to me, too." And then his dad, who loves him more than anything, rebukes him. The Hebrew word for "rebuke" that is used here is predominately used in the Old Testament when God is rebuking sinners. Jacob is saying, "What are you talking about? I'm not going to bow down to you! I'm your father! Who do you think you are?"

Jacob has created a monster, and the monster has turned against everyone. Joseph is arrogant. He's a liar. He's probably a blasphemer! Then he does one more thing. When Jacob needs to check on the brothers, he sends Joseph, the boy that they all hate, to them. When Joseph ends up in the pit, we can be tempted to think he's a victim—but we can read it another way and think, *I'd throw him in the pit, too.* When Joseph comes to his brothers, they strip him of his robe, the robe of many colors that he is wearing, and toss him into a pit. He inherits much baggage. He is a victim of circumstance. But he is also a victim of his own mistakes.

If we're honest, we admit that some of us aren't victims only of circumstance but also of our own mistakes. We're victims of our own shortcomings. Our lives are messes not because we've been born into the wrong families but because we have done the wrong things. We made them messes. But if Joseph can say, "All that was meant for evil, God meant it for good," we can see some powerful theology here. Joseph is saying, "I realize I made mistakes. I did things I shouldn't have. I participated in the evil, and yet somehow, in some way, God meant all of that for good." That means it is possible to have your life completely devastated by mistakes, to be sitting in the filth that you have created in your own life, and, at the same time, for God to have you exactly where he wants you while he is doing something amazing in your life. It is possible to be born into wrong situations and yet be used by, blessed by, and loved by God. It is also possible to make a mess of your own life and yet be used by, blessed by, and loved by God.

What Joseph I Thrown Into

The problems of his life are not only the ones Joseph is born into, and they are not only the ones he steps into; they are also the ones he is thrown into—quite literally. Joseph's brothers hate him. They hate Joseph for some reasons that have nothing to do with him. They hate him because he comes from the mom Jacob loves the most. They hate him because Dad loves him the most. They hate him for that coat. They hate him for the dreams. And yet the anger of Joseph's brothers is disproportionate to reality. Yes, their brother is arrogant. Yes, he lied about them. Yes, he wears that coat everywhere he goes. But he is seventeen. If we killed seventeen-year-olds for being stupid, we would not have many eighteen-year-olds. Hate, by its very nature, is seldom proportionate to what the person has actually done. Joseph is a victim of bitterness, hatred, and anger, and these things are going to crush him.

Generally speaking, there are two groups of people: those who are bitter toward someone else and those who are the victims of someone else's bitterness. Hate always tells us the problem is bigger than it actually is. That is what is going on here. Reuben is trying to reason with his brothers while Judah is trying to find a compromise. *Whether they kill him or sell him,* we think, *this is crazy. Why would you do this to your seventeen-year-old brother? What has he really done to deserve this?* They say they do it because they do not want his dreams to come true (Genesis 37:20). They fear what he might become, and they do not want to serve him. They are worried that Jacob is going to pull the same trick their father pulled and steal their blessing, which would make them all servants of Joseph.

What Joseph Grows Into

Joseph is born into a terrible situation—his father loves him as favorite and spoils him through no fault of his own—but he also steps into a million problems. He is an arrogant liar and he flaunts his jacket. He is then thrown into tremendous pain and difficulty due to the disproportionate hatred of his brothers. How does someone who has gone through all of that end up saying, "All that was meant for evil, God meant for good"? How does he come to that conclusion? He does not come to it overnight. He does not say that as he screams from the well. Imagine if the author wrote, "And Joseph shouted back while in the well, 'All that you are doing for evil, God is using for good.'" That doesn't happen. In chapter 37, Joseph is silent. Twenty years later, in Genesis 50, Joseph is saying, "I realize everything that has happened in my life—all that I was born into, all that I stepped into, all that I was thrown into—was God doing something good in my life."

The temptation is to think Joseph is saying, "Back when I knew you guys, way back in Genesis 37, I was so unlucky. But man, I went to Egypt, and boy, did my luck change!" But that is not what he says. It also would be easy for us to think (and a lot of bad books have been written about this) that Joseph could have said, "Hey! Back in Genesis 37, I was a moron. Then I went to Egypt and I learned these ten leadership principles. As I applied those principles to my life, everything got better. I have learned that if you have the right leadership principles, you can overcome anything." He does not say that, either. He says to his brothers, "As I look back, you were doing evil, I was doing evil, Dad was doing evil, and evil is never good, but even in all of our evil, the sovereign grace of God was doing something good."

Joseph comes to two conclusions: One, God loves him; two, God is using him. He says that God meant it all for good. Why would you do good to another person? Because you love them. In other words, Joseph says, "Because God loves me, he has meant it for good so that he might save people. Not only does God love me, he is using me. God loves me and he has a plan. I have a place in his great plan, and because of that, I am able to look back with perspective and say, 'Even though I was born into the exact wrong situation, I was really born into the right one. Even though I was born into a mess, I needed to step in it to get here. Even though I was thrown into a pit, I needed to be thrown into that to get here.'" When we come to the conclusion that God loves us and has a purpose for us and that he is going to use us in his purpose, everything starts to make sense. When we realize that the God we thought was against us is really for us, when we realize the God we thought was trying to kill us through difficult circumstances is actually trying to love us, we begin to look back over everything and we see it a new way.

Joseph goes back and says, "If I had not been born into that family, if I had not been arrogant and narcissistic, my brothers would not have thrown me in that well. If they had not thrown me in that well, I would never have gotten to Egypt." We are tempted to ask, "Why could God not have just dropped down and said, 'Joseph, go to Egypt'?" but what kind of Joseph would have gone to Egypt? Can you imagine Joseph walking into Pharaoh's palace, saying, "Pharaoh, I had a dream. Want to hear it?" He would have been killed for treason in an instant. We think that if God loves us, he would drop down and communicate to us without any pain or discomfort, but we overestimate our own ability to hear and to obey and listen. Joseph needed to be shaken up. He needed to be humbled and broken. Joseph is saying, "Now that I am where God has me, now that I know God loves me, I would not trade it for anything." He says to his brothers, "What you meant for evil, God meant for good," which translates into "Everything you think I hate, I love, because I see what God is doing."

The first step to living under God's sovereign grace is understanding, before we even begin to think about God, that he has been working in our lives. He is always working in and around what we are doing and what is being done to us. Whether our lives are being wrecked by circumstances, by ourselves, or by others, God is in that. But how do we know God loves us in the midst of our difficulties? How do we know God has a plan for us in our struggles? Joseph knows it because he has perspective. At the end of his life, he is in Egypt and he has saved everybody's life in the midst of a famine. If we could be heroes like that, then sure, we could love God. But we are not that type of hero.

We can know God loves us because thousands of years later, another young man was born into a hostile situation. That young man was Jesus. He was born into a hostile culture. The Roman Empire thought anybody with a monotheistic viewpoint was trouble to the state. Jesus was born under a Judaism that was all about external religion and not about an internal religion that changes the heart. The Jewish people wanted a Messiah, but they wanted a violent, political one. Jesus is born into difficulty, just like Joseph. He also steps into difficulty, but he does not do it like Joseph, with arrogance and narcissism. He steps into difficulty because he does not shy away from anything. On the Sabbath, he sees a man with a withered hand and the Jews lean in to see if Jesus is going to heal the man, because healing is not supposed to be done on the Sabbath. Jesus does it anyway, steps into difficulty. He says things like "Woe to you, scribes and Pharisees, hypocrites! For you are like whitewashed tombs, which outwardly appear beautiful, but within are full of dead people's bones and all uncleanness" (Matthew 23:27). He goes after the establishment. He goes after the heart. He says things like "You have heard that it was said to those of old, 'You shall not murder; and whoever murders will be liable to judgment.' But I say to you that everyone who is angry with his brother will be liable to judgment" (Matthew 5:21).

Jesus steps into difficulty, and then what do the brothers of his day do? They throw him into the pit of death. They put him on the cross and they crucify him. When they bring Jesus, Pilate says, "I will release Barrabbas who is a murderer, and a rebel, and a riot causer, or Jesus who heals people." The crowd says, "Crucify Jesus. We do not want Jesus" (Matthew 27:17–26). Jesus is thrown into "the pit" just like Joseph, but he does not stay dead; God the Father raises him from the dead. And Jesus does not say, "I hate you all; I am going to nuke this planet." Instead, his death, and the forgiveness it provides, is proof that

God loves us. Joseph had to wait until the end of his life to get that perspective, but Jesus says we do not have to wait, we can look to him. He says to us, "I was born into problems for you. I stepped into problems for you. I was thrown into problems for you. If you come to see I am not just a man, that I am the Son of God, and I went to the cross, where I paid for your sins, and I rose from the dead, then you will see that God loves you and he has a plan for you." Everyone who belongs to Christ by faith is in that plan.

We can ask, "If God really loves us enough to do all that, how can I be here? How can I be born into this? How could he have let me step into this? How could he let others throw me into this?" But don't we see we had to go through those things to get here? We think we would have listened anyway, but we would not have. What keeps bringing us back to God? Is it not the mess in which we live? God is using that mess to bring us to Jesus. If you are not a Christian, understand that the first step toward living out a relationship with God is coming to realize what Joseph came to realize: that God loves you, which he shows you through Jesus. Only then can you look back through your life and say, "All those times I thought God was not there, I now see God was bringing me to this moment to show me Christ."

We make Joseph a hero; we tell tales and sing songs about him. But Joseph was swept up in all this. He didn't choose to suffer. Suffering was thrust upon him. God did not come to him when he was twelve and say, "Here is the deal. I want you to be very arrogant. Then your brothers are going to hate you and throw you in a pit, but stick it out. It is going to be worth it." Joseph did not know his future, but Jesus knew his own future. He was in the garden on the night before his death, asking God, "Does it have to be this? Is there any other way?" God said, "No, there is no other way." Jesus said, "Okay. Let your will be done" (Luke 22:42). When we say, "If God loved me, he would not put me through this," God says, "Do you not see that because I love you, I went through something infinitely more painful and difficult than that for you? Yes, you had to go through that so you would listen to the suffering the Son went through on the cross."

If you are a Christian, there may be things in your life that cause bitterness toward God. Maybe it is time to look back over those things that have kept you from believing that God loves you. You can then ask, "God, is there something you are trying to teach me? Is there some corner in my heart that you do not have access to that you are trying to break?" If being broken is what it takes to get to God, it is infinitely worth it. Jesus came, endured, stepped, and was thrown into death for us, in order that through him, we might grow into a relationship with God. Only in Christ can we say that all this world meant for evil, God has meant for good.

Chapter 18

A Life Shaped by Sovereign Grace: Grace That Descends with Us

Genesis 39:1–21, 50:20

W e come to this text looking at Joseph's life and asking, "What does it look like to live a life under the sovereign grace of God?" Moses, the author of Genesis, has placed his story at the end of the book to show a man whose life was marked by God's grace. We can see how this grace moved throughout his life and how this same grace shaped him into a certain kind of man. We can look at Joseph and then look at our own lives and ask ourselves some challenging questions. The most challenging question would be "How does a man who was sold into slavery by his brothers then get promoted to a place power and influence, only to be framed for a crime and thrown into prison, become the kind of man who says, 'Everything in my life that was meant for evil, God meant for good'?"

When you look at the life of Joseph, what is amazing is not just about what he says at the end of his life, it is what he says during his life.

Throughout his life, Joseph rests and trusts in the sovereign grace of God, even though he lives a life that is a roller coaster of emotions and pain. Life has a ton of bad things to offer Joseph, yet he holds firm to his faith; he neither gets knocked off center nor is thrown into despair. This is not the case for many of us.

All of us are in the midst of difficulty or heading in that direction. There is a kind of cultural faith and worldview that has a deep and robust faith when life is good, but when life is difficult, that faith is easily shattered. Genesis 39 is here to teach us we can have a robust faith even when life is filled with difficult circumstances. How can we know God in such a deep and vibrant way that when we are the victims of terrible circumstances, we will not only still know God and still have a relationship with him but have faith that intensifies and doesn't shrink? How can we know God's grace not just when things are good but also when we are down in the depths? How do we have grace that descends with us so we are not alone in life's worst, most difficult moments?

Joseph's faith does not fall apart when he undergoes these circumstances because he simply does not believe lies about God that you and I believe so easily and subconsciously. It is the presence of these lies that wrecks us when we descend into the difficult circumstances. Joseph does not take the bait. The lies we believe are not just factual inaccuracies; instead, they are a kind of poison that, if we hold on to them, can ruin our lives. But if we can get past them, we will know God in a deep and robust way. These lies we believe are transactional, circumstantial, and universal.

The Transactional Lie

The transactional lie is the belief that we can conduct transactions with God: If you do everything right, then you can expect to get good things back; if you obey God, God will bless your circumstances and prosper you. When you read the first six verses of Genesis 39, it appears Joseph has that kind of relationship with God. Joseph is good at his job, and everything he does, the LORD blesses. God has given Joseph some natural abilities and gifts, and Joseph is flourishing in his role. Even though he is a slave from another country, he eventually rises to be the general manager of Potiphar's house. Everything that happens in Potiphar's house and estate is Joseph's doing. That means he is everything from a house manager to a financial planner to event coordinator to personal assistant. If Potiphar needs to get his wife flowers or buy a field, Joseph takes care of that. As if that were not enough, the writer of Genesis tells us, "Now Joseph was handsome in form and appearance" (Genesis 39:6b). It is not enough that the guy is really good at his job; he is also really good-looking, very muscular, and very strong. He is a front-cover-of-the-magazine kind of guy.

We all want that kind of life. We want to be healthy, wealthy, and, if it would not be too much to ask, good-looking. As long as we have all of those things, it becomes very easy to believe in God. It is very easy to celebrate a God who gives us health, wealth, happiness, and good looks, isn't it?

Joseph does everything that is right. He works hard, he gives his best effort, he plans, and he takes care of himself. Did we say he is handsome in form and appearance? It is tempting to believe that because he does what is right, God gives him what is right. That is the transactional understanding of God: As long as I do well, I am rewarded. That is how we think it works. Seldom do we think this consciously, but subconsciously, we are keeping score and thinking that as long as we are good people, God will bless us.

There are two tests for whether we believe the transactional lie. One test is negative and one test is positive. First, the negative test—when you are doing your religious duties like coming to church, praying, serving, and reading scripture, do you think to yourself that you are doing it because you are supposed to do it? Where does that idea come from? Why do we use the language of "supposed to" and "should"? When we say we are supposed to go to church, we are saying, "My end of the equation is going to church. This is what I do for

God." There is an expectation of reciprocity when we complete our *shoulds* and *oughts* and *supposed tos*. Next, the positive test—when life goes wrong for us, is our first inclination to say it is not fair? Are we tempted to say it is not fair because we really mean we do not deserve things going wrong? When we say we don't deserve it, we believe we have done good things and that when we do good things, we are supposed to get good things in return. But when we look at the story of Joseph, we see that thinking is absolutely, unequivocally false. When you do the right thing, you are not always going to get the best in return. Potiphar's wife begins to cast her eyes on Joseph, and she is persistent in her seduction. Most commentators will agree she is pursuing him daily until she grabs him and says, "Now! Lie with me," and he has to run away.

Every moment, he does the right thing. In fact, Potiphar's wife uses only two words in the Hebrew, and Joseph's response to her is thirty-five Hebrew words. He is not just moral; he is thoughtful. He does everything right, and yet, even at the crucial moment when he is more right than ever, his life completely falls apart. He does the right thing, but he gets the wrong thing. He does good, but he gets evil. What are we to make of this?

The transactional view of God is not only not true, but it also does violence to Joseph and robs him of his person. If Joseph were going to have a relationship with God in which God kept score, then God could not love in any kind of dynamic way but only in a static way. God could not lavish his love on Joseph. He would have to wait for Joseph to do something good. God would not be a loving, personal God for Joseph; rather, he would be a reward. The transactional view of God does violence to God because it strips God of any ability to be personal, of any ability to be individual, of any ability to make choices as he sees fit. The transactional lie is the opposite of what is going on here, because the text says the LORD was with Joseph, yet, he is not doing that dependent upon Joseph as though God is the puppet and Joseph is the puppeteer. God is with Joseph independent of who Joseph is, what Joseph does, or where Joseph goes.

The transactional view does not just do violence to God by turning him into a puppet God but also does violence to us. If we hold to the view that when we do good, we get good, that view is the opposite of grace. If God really is transactional, then there cannot be any such thing as grace. In this passage, Joseph does everything right, but the problem is, how does Joseph end up in Egypt in the first place? He is an arrogant, spoiled teenager who shoves his promised future in every-body's face. His family hates him so much that they sell him into slavery and he ends up in Egypt. He may be doing everything right here, but he was not doing everything right earlier. If God were keeping score, in Genesis 39:2, we would not read, "The LORD was with Joseph." The Lord would not have been with Joseph because he would not have earned his presence.

The difficulty of the transactional view is that if we say, "If I do right, I get right," we tend to only focus on the "right" things and ignore the "wrong" things. If God is up in heaven keeping score, then he is not just making note of when we do right but is also making note of when we do wrong. If we knew ourselves well enough, we would have to admit that at least we have wrongs canceling out our rights. We have way more wrong than right. That means we have a negative balance with God, meaning he owes us not blessing but punishment.

It is important to note that God is not punishing Joseph. In Joseph's life, the initial hope of God's sovereign grace is that the LORD is with him independent of his deserving for God to be there. The story of Joseph, like all stories in Genesis, is the story of God being with some-one who does not deserve it, bringing good into their lives they do not deserve, and using them in a way they do not deserve. Joseph's story is really no different than Jacob's, Isaac's, Abraham's, Noah's, Seth's, and the rest. God does not deal in transactions. Just because we do what is right on occasion does not mean we are always going to get good things in life.

The Circumstantial Lie

If God does not deal in transactions, then why does Joseph go through these circumstances? The circumstantial lie says that if we endure difficult circumstances, it is because God does not have a plan and has abandoned us. We do not consciously think this, but it is what we are actually thinking. When life goes bad and we endure difficult circumstances, the cry of our hearts is "How could God let this happen? If this is happening to me, it must mean that God does not love me," yet Joseph's story tells us that is clearly not true.

Joseph does endure difficult circumstances. He is sold into slavery, pursued by a powerful woman who tells lies about him, thrown into jail, and abandoned. Joseph is under incredibly difficult circumstances, yet verse 21 says the Lord was with Joseph and showed him steadfast love. The difficult circumstances of Joseph's life do not mean that God does not love him. They do not mean God has given up on him. The fact that Joseph's plan deviates from what Joseph wanted or what Joseph thought was best does not mean that God does not care about him. In fact, it indicates the opposite.

When we believe our lives are good because God loves us and our lives are bad because God has abandoned us, we are doing violence to God and violence to ourselves through believing the circumstantial lie. Do we want a robotic God? Do we want a God who says, "What can I do for you today?" or do we want a God who loves us with some personality? We obviously want a God who loves us dynamically, who sees us in a particular way, and who loves us in a particular way. In the same way, no two marriages are alike, because marriages are made of individuals, God desires to love us in a way he sees as best, not necessarily in a way we see as best. God is loving Joseph as God sees fit, and that is enough for Joseph.

The circumstances we think are best are not always best. The life we want is not always the life that is best. Joseph did not wish for these circumstances, yet this is part of the path of God to make him the second most powerful man in Egypt. We cannot say to God, "Why is my life going this way?" because we only have a two-foot vision of our lives. He has an aerial view of our lives. He knows what he is doing. For most of us, the absolute worst thing God could do is give us what we want. If God had said to Joseph, "What can I do for you today?" Joseph would have said, "Take me back to my family." If God had done that, his family would have starved. Although we never want difficult circumstances in life, and although we often have no idea what is going on, sometimes what is best for us are the difficult circumstances.

We evaluate the circumstances of our lives and whether they are good or bad by running them through the prism of our end goal. At the same time, we want to be loved by a God who has an end goal for us that is bigger than our two-foot vision. If we truly want this, then it is likely that when we view circumstances through his eternal prism instead of our shortsighted prism, the circumstances we thought were bad were actually for our good, and, to take it a step further, maybe the ones we thought would have been good actually would have been bad. Imagine marrying the person you used to love, only now they make you cringe. When Joseph says, "The things in my life that were meant for evil, God meant for good," it is like he is saying, "I never would have ended up here if I had not gone through those things. Now that I see what God was doing, I look back over my life and I see I absolutely needed those things."

The Universal Lie

Not only is it a lie to say that if we do right, then we get right, and not only is it a lie to say that God only loves us if our lives go the way we want them to go, but when we believe both of those lies, they combine to form a third lie that says anyone who goes through difficulty should stop believing. This lie drives a lot of people to atheism. But here in the midst of great difficulty, you have Joseph, who does not lose his faith. In prison, Joseph asks God for interpretations to other prisoners' dreams, which means he has not lost his faith in God (Genesis 40). He keeps his faith in the one true God in the midst of a polytheistic society. He still talks to God, and he still believes God will use him. His faith is not rattled. Joseph is a sign to us that, although we go through very difficult situations, although we often think God owes us and does not come through, we can still believe. Joseph does, and Joseph is not an outlier. He is not a robotic dude who questions his faith.

In Genesis 50:25, Joseph tells his brothers that one day, God is going to take them out of Egypt into the promised land and fulfill all his promises. Joseph asks his family to take his bones with them when that day comes. He is saying, "My whole life has been pinned to the hope that God made a promise and that he keeps his promises. That means we are going to end up in Canaan, not in Egypt, so when you leave Egypt, take my bones with you." This is the only hope for Joseph's life when all is said and done. When Joseph was being dragged to prison, he was thinking, *God made a promise. God keeps his promises. One day, all of this will be made right through my God, who told Abraham he is going to put the world back together. Even if I cannot see it impact my circumstances now, my hope is that one day it will happen.* Joseph does not believe the transactional or circumstantial lies but rather believes in the promise of the story of God. Joseph is not saying, "It is my story." Rather, he is saying, "It is your story, God. I do not know how this all fits in, but my hopes are pinned to your story."

God's promise to Abraham comes partly true in the life of Joseph. Joseph blesses the nations by taking care of them and providing food for them. God shows us that his promise is beginning to happen with Joseph but it does not happen completely. Joseph tells his family to take his bones with them because he knows the promise has yet to be realized. He is looking forward to somebody else, and that somebody else is Jesus.

Jesus would come and always do what was right. In some areas of our lives, we can be very moral and say no to sin, but in other areas of our lives, we are very weak. Joseph is like us. Joseph struggled and was able to face down sexual temptation, but his pride and manipulation landed him in that very situation. In Genesis 39, he is very heroic, but in Genesis 37, he is an idiot that everybody hates. Jesus always did what was right, yet very few times in his life did he get what was right in a transactional sense. He did not have a home. His friends deserted him when he needed them the most. He endured his most difficult circumstances when he was falsely accused, arrested, beaten, and crucified. Throughout all of this, Jesus never lost his faith. He never said, "God, I hate you. I am out. I am over this. I am not going to do this." He was obedient, even to the point of death on the cross.

If you struggle with sexual temptation and you think, *I can never break free of pornography,* then that is a lie you tell yourself. We know it is a lie because Joseph walked away from that temptation. In that way, Joseph convicts and condemns us, but Jesus convicts us in all things. Everything he says, everything he does not say, everything he does, and everything he does not do convicts and condemns us. His actions show us that the problem is us, not God. Even after Jesus on the cross says, "My God! My God! Why have you forsaken me?" he says, "Father, into your hands I commit my spirit" (Luke 23:46). Jesus does not give up on God, yet you and I give up on God when our health deteriorates, our bank accounts evaporate, and our relationships fall apart. The problem is not God, it is us. We want what we want when we want it. We want our stories, our circumstances, and our plans. Joseph is imperfectly saying what Jesus says with perfection: "I want your plan, Father. I trust your plan."

The good news of Jesus is not that his faithfulness condemns our faithlessness. When he rises from the dead, he writes a different story by saying to us, "I went to the cross and God turned his back to me and crucified me. He crucified me for all your transactional lies and all your circumstantial lies. I died for all of that—all of your anger, all of your hatred, all of your faithlessness. I rose from the dead so you would know that, although God may bring difficult circumstances, he always resurrects." Jesus is showing us that what God breaks, he builds back up. God broke Jesus but built him back up. He killed Jesus but raised him back up. Even though we think God is breaking us and destroying us, he is doing it that he might build us back up. Jesus paid for all the lies we believe about God, all the violence we have done to God, ourselves, and others. By rising from the dead, Jesus is saying we can be forgiven in him and that in him, we might come to know God in such a way that we can hold firm in the depths of life. Joseph does it because he believes in the promise of God's story. When he says, "Take my bones," to whom is he looking? He is looking to Jesus—the fulfillment of God's story of redemption.

Jesus calls us to trust that God is writing a story to fix the world and we can be a part of this story. First, we must admit that we have been angry with God but that the problem is not God and we are the ones that have been faithless. Joseph and Jesus show us that we are the problem. From here, we can turn to Jesus. But if we put our trust in Jesus, does it mean we will not have difficult circumstances? No. We absolutely will have difficulties. Jesus, the one in whom the story is fulfilled, lived a life of difficult circumstances. Does it mean you will always get what you think you deserve? No. The Son of God prayed for God to remove the cup of suffering that he didn't deserve, but the Father said no. Trusting in Jesus will mean that in the darkest moments, the Lord will be with us. We will know, just like Joseph, that God is writing a story in the world and that it will be fulfilled.

The call for us all, Christian and non-Christian alike, is to exit our stories and walk toward the story of God. The call of faith is to say, "I do not deserve to be in this story, but because of what Jesus has done, I can be brought into it." When we know God, who are we to ask, "How can you let me go through this?" It is his story. He has promised that in the end, he will make all things new. In whose story do you want to live? You can choose your own. You can have a transactional, circumstantial, and universal view of God in which God gives you what you want and if he does not give you what you want, you take your ball and go home. You will be robbing yourself of any kind of real relationship with God and of any kind of life with purpose and meaning. Or you can say, "God, I do not know what you are doing; I do not understand it. I have questions, but I am going to trust." And if you find yourself at a place where you cannot trust anymore, look to Jesus. If God fulfilled all of this with the crucifixion of his own Son and gave him up for us, then do we really think he is not going to follow through with our troubles? He will follow through, and he has proven it in Christ.

Chapter 19

Grace That Gives a Better Story

Genesis 39:1–12 50:25

At this point in Genesis, Joseph is a young person in the beginning stages of his vocational work and he is rising up the ladder. He begins his life as a slave doing menial things, but doing those things very well. He moves up in rank until he is overseeing everything in Potiphar's house. But even with all this outward success, Joseph comes to this place, where he is tempted in a powerful way. Potiphar's wife desires to seduce Joseph into an affair, so she propositions him every day. She gets increasingly provocative and seductive each day until she clears the house of all the other people, and traps Joseph when he is wearing only his inner garment. Potiphar's wife grabs him, saying, "Sleep with me."

Joseph has come to one of those moments that happen in all of our lives, and he has to determine whether he is going to succumb to temptation or resist temptation. The amazing thing is … Joseph does resist. So many of us give in, but Joseph does not. The temptation does not have to be sex, per se. It could be the temptation to be greedy, it could be pride, or it could be other things, but sexual temptation is one of the most powerful forms of temptation. Potiphar's wife is right there in front of Joseph. and she wants him now, but he does not give in, and his life continues on the trajectory that God has for it. For Joseph to resist, there has got to be something Joseph understands that we do not, and if we could understand it, theoretically, we too could get through these moments of temptation. We could thrive and flourish instead of die beneath the consequences of poor choices.

Joseph, as we remember, was not always a stand-up guy. When we read Genesis 37, we see Joseph as a very arrogant, obnoxious young guy who sticks his dreams in people's faces. When he visits his brothers, who hate him, he wears his special coat to show them that he is still the favorite son. Joseph has not always been able to overcome temptation, and yet here he does.

So what has changed? What has he learned? And why does it matter? It is incredibly relevant because either you are in one of those moments right now or you will eventually get there. Either way, we need to learn from Joseph. We need to ask what Joseph understands that we do not.

Joseph's Awareness

In verse 9, Joseph says something many of us might blow right past. He is talking to Potiphar's wife. She only says two words in the Hebrew to him in her request for sex. He says thirty-five words back to her, but he ends with, "How then can I do this great wickedness and sin against God?" Joseph is telling her that to sleep with her is fundamentally not about him and her and it is not about him and Potiphar. It is primarily about Joseph and God. He is saying that to do this would be to sin against God primarily. Depending on our upbringing and beliefs, we might misunderstand this verse. We may see Joseph as a fundamentalist who actually believes God cares about what goes on in our bedrooms, or we can see Joseph as a model rule follower: Joseph is right and there is a rule and he must keep it to be accepted by God. It does not matter if he knows why the rule is wrong, it is simply wrong, so he does not do it. But we cannot understand Genesis 39 until we understand what Joseph is saying in verse 9. If we read this religiously (as a rule follower) or irreligiously (Joseph is such a prude!), we are going to miss what is going on.

To understand this passage, we need two things. First, we need to know what the Bible means when it defines sin. If we take an irreligious view, we tend to think of one person imposing their morality on someone else. If we take a religious view, we see sin as pertaining to a rule we must keep. If we break the rule, that is sin. If we keep the rule, that is good. Neither of those are good definitions of sin, according to the Bible. To get a better definition, we have to go back to the beginning of Genesis. In Genesis 1, God creates a perfect environment for human flourishing. In chapter 2, he creates a garden, and rests Adam and Eve in the garden. He creates a place where they can flourish and be nourished. He then gives them the best job description ever—to create, cultivate, shape, mold, build, and study.

Then God puts a tree in the middle of the garden. He tells Adam and Eve, "Do not eat from the tree, or you are going to die." God does not mean the tree is poisonous. We know that because they do eat from the tree, and they do not keel over. God is also not keeping the tree for himself. Instead, God is saying the only way the perfect environment could be disrupted is if we reject it in favor of another story. Every time Adam and Eve walk past the tree in the garden and do not eat from it, they are saying they are happy to be in God's plan and that the story God is writing is sufficient for them. The presence of the tree indicates that although they are in the story, they are not the main characters of the story. That belongs to God. And when the serpent comes up to tempt them, he offers them a story in which they are the main characters and suggests that God is actually holding back from them. He says the story God is crafting for them is lacking. When they eat the fruit, they are agreeing with Satan and not God. They are rejecting God's story for a different story.

That is fundamentally what the Bible means when it talks about sin: Sin is rejecting the story of God in favor of another story, and every time we sin, we are saying we would rather be in a different story than God's story. When we sin against God, the fundamental problem is not that we have broken a rule. The fundamental problem is saying to God that we want a story in which we are the center. That is what Adam and Eve said, and that is what Potiphar's wife is offering to Joseph.

Joseph recognizes that the story Potiphar's wife is offering is not better than the one God is writing. If we look forward to Genesis 50, we see Joseph talking with his brothers, getting ready to die, saying that God's story is not about him. God is still doing something even though Joseph is getting ready to die, and Joseph asks his brothers to take his bones with them when God does it. What has empowered Joseph to keep his faith despite being thrown in a pit, then sold into slavery, being falsely accused of rape, and being imprisoned is that Joseph understands God is doing something and that he wants to be part of it. Even if it means Joseph is only bones, he would rather be dead bones in God's story than the highest guy in Egypt. He is saying to Potiphar's wife that the story she is offering is inadequate compared to the one God is writing. Joseph understands God is restoring the world through his family, and that is what he wants. Potiphar's wife cannot offer that. Joseph is making an strategic decision. What is superior—to be a part of God's story or to be part of her story of sexual temptation? Joseph is not going to work every day willing himself not to sleep with Potiphar's wife. Rather, he is going to work every day reminding himself that God is doing something, that God has made a promise and keeps his promises.

Joseph's Argument

Joseph makes two arguments—one positive and one negative—and since he spends more time on the positive argument than the negative, so will we. Joseph says the goodness of God's story is superior to any other story. Verse 8 says, "But he refused and said to his master's wife,

'Behold! Because of me, my master has no concern about anything in the house, and he has put everything that he has in my charge. He is not greater in this house than I am, nor has he kept anything from me.'" He is making a micro- and a macro argument here. The micro argument is this: He has been doing everything God's way, and things are going really well. Yes, he is still a slave, but other than that, he has experienced nothing but good. When Joseph was bought as a slave, Potiphar did not choose him intending to make him a manager. Joseph started doing menial grunt work, but at every stop, Joseph excelled. God was with him, blessing him. Joseph sees what God is doing in his life, and he will not trade that for moments of pleasure. On the micro level, the goodness of God in his life is superior to sexual satisfaction. For some of us, sexual satisfaction is of little enticement, but for others, the thought that anything could be better than sexual satisfaction is paradigm-shifting. Joseph says it is possible to know the grace of God and see it in such a way that we would not pursue illicit sexual satisfaction. To give up what God is doing for that would be to give up something better for something less.

Joseph is also making a macro argument, though not explicitly. In a few moments, Potiphar's wife will accuse him of rape and throw him in prison, where he will stay for a long time, yet even in prison, when Joseph engages with his fellow inmates, he talks about the faithfulness of God. On a micro level, God's plan is looking terrible while Joseph is sitting in prison, but on a macro level, Joseph recognizes that God's plan is continuing on like a freight train. In Genesis 50:25, he understands God is doing something. He knows his family will not stay in Egypt but will go to Canaan and be a blessing to the nations because that is what God promised to Abraham. When they depart for Canaan, Joseph asks his family to take his bones with them. He will be dead, not participating, but it will be enough for his bones to be somewhere in the story. He wants to be around what God is doing, which is bigger than him.

Joseph resists sin by making an argument for God's goodness. Joseph is not arguing with Potiphar's wife to get her to understand that sin is wrong and God will punish them. Instead, he says that there is a superior plan that he is choosing. Joseph, and Christianity as a whole, argues against evil with the power of beauty. Hebrews 11:6 says, "Without faith it is impossible to please [God], for whoever would draw near to God must believe that God exists and that he rewards those who seek him." If we really want to meet God, we must go looking for him, believing he is there, and we must believe that it is going to be good if we find him. What ultimately drives Christian faith is the belief in the superiority of God's goodness, yet most of us do not try to argue ourselves out of sin—we try to will ourselves out of it. That is not true Christianity; that is some other masochistic religion. Christianity says, "Come to know God in such a way that the thought of putting God down for anything else is an idiotic thought." The Gospel is fighting evil with beauty, and Joseph is saying there are so many beautiful things God is doing, why would he trade it for a sexual encounter?

There is another story in the Bible in which a man continually lusts after a woman until he traps and rapes her. When he is done with his deed, he hates her. He desires her so fiercely, he rapes her, but when he gets what he wants, he hates it (2 Samuel 13). This cycle of lust and hatred is true for so many of us. We want something so badly, and then when we get it, we hate it. Do we know God in such a way that his beauty is our argument against stepping outside of his story? Do we fight sin with masochism and self-hatred, or do we fight it with beauty? Do we meditate on the law of the Lord? Is our delight in it? Do we find goodness there? Is that goodness the argument against wickedness? The difference between the wicked and the righteous are those who have become consumed with the goodness of God and those who have rejected it in favor of another story.

We cannot fight sin with self-hatred, muttering, snapping rubber bands on our wrists, or Internet filters. We must replace sin with something beautiful. Joseph is telling us he has found something better. Many of us have family members that are eaten up with so many sins—it could be greed, pride, drug addiction, pornography, etc.—and if we sit with them and say, "What are you doing? You are so stupid!" we are not helping them at all. The Christian can look at them and ask, "Do you not see there is something so much better than what you're chasing?" Jesus says the kingdom of heaven is like a man who finds a treasure in a field who joyfully goes to sell all he has to buy the field (Matthew 13:44). Along the way, people probably ask him what he is thinking, selling everything for a dumb field, but he knows what they do not: In the field is the greatest treasure. To those on the outside, it looks like he is making an inferior choice, but he is not. He is making a superior choice. That is a positive argument to avoid sin.

There is also a negative argument. Joseph's negative argument lies in verse 9, where he says, "He is not greater in this house than I am, nor has he kept back anything from me except you, because you are his wife." We have an ethic in our culture that says nothing is wrong unless it hurts somebody, yet here Joseph says to Potiphar's wife, "You can clear the house out. You can tell me nobody is ever going to know, but this is going to hurt Potiphar. It is going to hurt you, and it is going to hurt me." Simply put, Joseph is saying that to step outside of God's story is to always bring violence into the world. Every other story fuels violence. It does not have to be an overt violence. The violence can be relational, existential, or emotional, but all kinds of violence come about when we step outside of God's story.

Joseph's Action

Joseph's arguments lead him to action. In today's culture, Joseph is most famous for running away. Verse 11 says, "But one day, when he went into the house to do his work and none of the men of the house were there in the house, she caught him by his garment, saying, 'Lie with me.' But he left his garment in her hand and fled and got out of the house." Most commentators believe he ran out naked, or very close to naked. He ran with reckless abandon, not worrying about what other people thought or wondering about the conclusions they might draw. He just understood that he had to get out of there. When we read this passage and place it in the context of Genesis and the story of Joseph's life, we realize Joseph is not ultimately running away from something as much as he is running toward something. Yes, in a sense, he is running away because to run toward anything is to run away from something else. He is running away from Potiphar's wife, but he runs to the superiority of God's story. When she grabs him and says, "I do not care about God's story. I want to write a different story right now," he runs away from her but toward God's story. Genesis 50:25 tells us that Joseph, through his whole life, in every situation, has been running toward God's story. He has been saying, "I do not want to be the main character in some fleeting story. I want to be a part, even if it is dead bones, of what God is doing in the history of the world." If we spend our lives only trying to run away, we will never get very far. If we have something to run toward, we will make it. This is Joseph's path.

Joseph resists, he argues for something better, and then he runs. In this story, he comes up a hero, yet in Genesis 37, when tempted by pride and arrogance, when he had dreams and he rubbed them in his brothers' faces, Joseph was not so heroic. Joseph came to understand that God is writing a story and although he was a part of it, he was not the central character of the story. That is why he says, "When God writes the rest of the story, take my bones with you. I want to be in God's story even if I am only a pile of bones." Where does this story ultimately lead? If not Joseph, who? Who is the one to whom his bones will be carried?

Ultimately, Joseph is talking about Jesus. Jesus is a descendent of Abraham, the one through whom God said he would fix the world. While Jesus was on Earth, he was always living in God's story. Jesus did nothing of his own but did only what he saw his Father doing (John 5:19–20). When tempted in the desert, Jesus responds to Satan with "It is written," meaning "I will not give in to your story. God's story has been written, and that is the story in which I choose to live." Jesus is so in God's story that when he was being baptized, the heavens opened and God said, "This is my son, in whom I am well pleased"

(Matthew 3:17). Jesus walks in God's story, and because he walks in God's story, he never does violence. Everywhere he goes, people flourish, lives are put back together, the dead are raised, the sick are healed, and the lame walk. Everywhere he goes, Jesus rejects any other narrative outside the story of God's redemptive grace. Even when Pilate says, "Do you not understand I have the power to make you live or die?" Jesus answers, "You only have the power God gives you. It is God's story, Pilate. It is not yours" (John 19:11).

When we understand that sin is rejecting the narrative God is writing and creating our own narrative, we will see that sin is not about breaking rules but about spending our whole life creating stories that do not work while we turn our back on God. Once we see this, we can understand that the only thing we should expect from God is judgment, yet Jesus, who has always been in God's story, who has always known relationship with God, goes to the cross for sinners, and on the cross, he says, "My God! My God! Why have you forsaken me?" (Matthew 27:46). Why does Jesus cry out this prayer? He is saying, for the first time in the history of the world, that someone in the Godhead stepped outside the story of God because we were outside God's story. As he is hanging on the cross, he is hanging there for every time we have chased our own stories in regards to sexuality, money, pride, and arrogance—and the list can go on and on. Every narrative we have created, every other story we have wanted, Jesus bears on the cross.

On the cross, Jesus is willingly giving himself up for the church, and when he rises from the dead, he says to us, "Trust me. Believe that on the cross, your narratives are being punished and I receive the punishment. Believe that the only way back into God's story is to say that the judgment you rightfully deserve has been put on me. Now you can be forgiven and accepted. Now you can be brought back into God's story."

Adam began the human story and catapulted us into sin, but God sent a second Adam, Jesus, and he has started a new story (Romans 5). All of us live in one of those stories—the story of sin or the story of God. Adam's story has seven billion variations that we create daily. God's story has one version that Jesus created. Every other religion says that if you want to get back in God's story, you need to pull yourself up by your bootstraps, you need to hate yourself, and you should hate what you do that is evil. Christianity says if you want to get back in God's story, the only thing that can trump your evil is God's beauty—and God's beauty is most displayed in Christ, who gave himself up for you on the cross. The only hope we have of being dead bones in God's story is God becoming dead bones for us. Our only hope is that God is writing a story. Sometimes we will see it on the micro level; sometimes we will not. Sometimes we will have to lean on the macro level that God is changing the world through Jesus. This is our hope.

Some of us might need to put down the story we are writing and pick up, for the first time ever, the story God is writing through Jesus. Others of us, as Christians, are not just proclaiming what Christ has done but are proclaiming what he is still doing. It is not enough to say, "Yes, I believe God died for me, but I still want to hold on to my stories of sexual fulfillment, career aspirations, and life goals." Rather, we can say, "My only hope of being set free from my story is that I might know God through the person of Jesus in such an intimate and beautiful way that everything else might grow pale."

There is an old hymn that says, "Turn your eyes upon Jesus. Look full in his wonderful face, and the things of earth will grow strangely dim in the light of his glory and grace." Have we ever asked the Lord to make Jesus so beautiful that our addictions, infidelities, personal comforts, and pride grow dim? Do we believe there is a better story for us in Christ? How do we know this story is better? Because in our story, we are currently being destroyed, and in the other story, God was destroyed for us.

Chapter 20

Grace That Enables Reconciliation

Genesis 45:1–15, 50:15–21

When Joseph comes face-to-face with his brothers, his response is difficult for us to comprehend. The idea that Joseph would confront those who had sinned against him and would forgive them is incredibly difficult to understand. It becomes particularly difficult if our own lives can be traced back to a single traumatic event or a series of traumatic events at the hands of someone else. If we can trace our stories back to someone who violated us, oppressed us, or made life difficult for us and we read this story through that lens of pain, it is very easy to look at Joseph as a robot who mindlessly forgives because the Bible says he has to forgive. Though the story is hard to comprehend, it is extremely relevant to us because life is about relationships—professional, personal, family, romantic, and neighborly. No matter what sphere of life we are talking about, it can be connected to relationships, and in our broken world, where everything seems to be falling apart, life is often about damaged relationships and trying to navigate through the difficulty of being in relationships with people who hurt us, or the difficulty of being in relationships with people we have hurt.

There is a temptation when we hear the story of the Bible to put ourselves in the character's shoes. It is very easy to want to be just like Joseph, who endures life's difficult circumstances and who maintains a healthy perspective on life. Who wouldn't want to be the one who rises to power in Egypt and saves the world with his ingenuity? It is easy to want that kind of faith when we can look backwards on life, but the test for any worldview is this: Is it really going to allow me to navigate through the world in the present tense?

We are a mess, and we need a worldview that both makes sense of the world and can make sense of us. Can it help us navigate the world while we're in the mess? Can it help us encounter, endure in, and flourish within a world of fractured relationships? That is a good test for any worldview or religion. It is a good test for Genesis, and it is a good test for Joseph. How does Joseph's story help us put together the pieces of our lives? We have a guy who simultaneously is difficult to understand, particularly if we have been victims in any real sense of the word, but also has faith that gives him the ability to forgive the most heinous of crimes. This perspective is the exact thing that we need if we are going to thrive and flourish in a world where relationships are broken.

The Significance of Joseph's Forgiveness

Joseph's brothers sinned against him greatly, and as we know, it is generally easier to forgive small things than bigger things. In the world, there is an unspoken sliding scale on the forgiveness meter. Cutting someone off in traffic is one thing, but killing their family is another. So if there were a scale, Joseph would be at the extreme end of things. From the time he was thrown into a pit by his brothers to the time he is in power under Pharaoh, thirteen years of his life have passed, simply because his brothers hated the fact that he was an obnoxious teenager and because he flaunted his coat.

The temptation when we have been hurt, when we are victims, is to read a passage like this and say, "This does not apply to me. If you knew what was done to me, how often it was done, you would know I could never forgive." On a human level, that makes absolute sense. If we are at such a place, we need to see that Joseph does identify with us. He lost thirteen years of his life. He was sold into slavery by his own brothers. He was falsely accused of rape and imprisoned for a crime he didn't commit. He was significantly sinned against.

Not only did his brothers sin against Joseph greatly, but when Joseph sees them again decades later, they are not sorry and they have not changed. In Genesis 50, Jacob dies and the brothers worry that Joseph has been secretly waiting for his father to die so he can have them killed. After Jacob dies, they send a message to Joseph: "Your father gave this command before he died: 'Say to Joseph, "Please forgive the transgression of your brothers and their sin, because they did evil to you." And now, please forgive the transgression of the servants of the God of your father'" (Genesis 50:16–17). "Servants of God" is not a phrase we would normally use in relation to Joseph's brothers. Some other names can come to mind, but "servants of God" is probably not one of them. Also, Jacob never, to our knowledge, knows the full story of what his brothers did. Because of this, most commentators say the brothers are lying. The brothers are still manipulating to the very end of the story. They manipulate after Joseph has taken care of them and forgiven them.

Joseph's response is to weep. He weeps because his brothers have not changed at all. Most of us can only find it in ourselves to forgive someone who is sorry. We can extend forgiveness to the one who is willing to change and who comes to us, hat in hand, and admits their fault. But what about the person who is not sorry, the one who does not recognize their fault? That person is very hard to forgive. Joseph has eleven people like this. They are still lying, still manipulating, still betraying. They have not changed.

Joseph's forgiveness is significant on many levels. What makes his situation most unique is that he has had the rare opportunity to destroy those who have sinned against him. Twice. The first opportunity is in chapter 45. The famine is in full effect and the brothers come hungry, looking to Joseph for food. Joseph reveals himself, and they are terrified. When we have been deeply sinned against, don't we all daydream about the moment when we can get payback, the moment when we have power? Joseph has the opportunity to crush the people who destroyed him. They ruined thirteen years of his life, and now he has the guys in front of him who have caused this and he has the opportunity to kill them with the backing of the entire legal system at his disposal. Joseph is the number-two guy in Egypt. If he calls Pharaoh and says, "These guys are bothering me," then his brothers are going to die. He also has the opportunity to throw them in prison for, say, thirteen years. He has the opportunity to lie to them and to see them undergo the same manipulation that caused his difficulties. Joseph has a chance to sell them into slavery. He has the opportunity that we always wish we had. Some of us spend every day daydreaming about retaliation because our lives have been so wrecked by someone that we wish we had the chance to wreck their lives. Joseph actually has that moment twice, in Genesis 45 and again in Genesis 50, and he forgives.

The Source of Joseph's Forgiveness

Joseph gives three reasons for his forgiveness. They are not really three separate things but one sentence in three parts. First, he says God has a cosmic plan. When Joseph reveals himself to his brothers in chapter 45 and says, "It is me," he says, "Do not be distressed or angry with yourselves because you sold me here, for God sent me" (Genesis 45:5). Again, he tells them, "God sent me here" (Genesis 45:8). Finally, he tells them again, "So it was not you who sent me here, but God. He has made me a father to Pharaoh. As for you, you meant evil against me, but God meant it for good" (Genesis 50:20). Joseph's first argument for forgiveness lies in him trusting God's cosmic plan. In other words, Joseph is saying, "Over the years, I have learned to look at the macro story of God and see what God is doing. This allows me a deep peace when I view the micro details of my life. In my life, I have chosen to emphasize the macro idea that God has a cosmic plan, and the micro things you have done cannot derail that plan."

Not only does God have a plan, but his brothers' sin was actually a part of God's plan. This is a difficult concept to grasp, but let's try. If God has a plan for evil, is sin truly evil? Joseph says, in Genesis 45:4, "I am your brother, Joseph, whom you sold into Egypt." He does not mitigate their guilt at all. Later on, he says to his brothers, "As for you, you meant evil against me" (Genesis 50:20). Joseph is fully aware of the evil they intended. Remember the beginning of the story, when he is in the pit, screaming for help while they are eating lunch? He is not under any illusion as to who his brothers are or what they were trying to do, yet look at how he comforts them: "And now do not be distressed or angry with yourselves ... for God sent me before you to preserve life. ... God sent me before you to preserve a remnant. ... So it was not you who sent me here, but God" (Genesis 45:5–8). Not only does God have a plan, but he uses the brothers' evil, hatred, and betrayal to execute the plan and get Joseph to Egypt. When Joseph says, "It was not you who sent me here, but God," he means God sent him through the evil of his brothers. He is able to forgive them because he understands that God has a cosmic plan and in his cosmic plan, he uses their evil to accomplish good things. The brothers were evil, but they were the instrument that got Joseph to Egypt. Because he can see God's sovereignty, Joseph has changed the way he sees his brothers. He understands they are a necessary component of God's cosmic plan.

Joseph sees that God has a story, sees that his brothers' evil is part of that story, and, finally, understands that God is using their own evil to rescue them. Genesis 45:7 says, "God sent me before you to preserve for you a remnant on earth, and to keep alive for you many survivors." Joseph is saying, "God is using your evil for your good." Look ahead to Genesis 45:10, where the author writes, "You shall dwell in the land of Goshen. You shall be near me. You and your children and your children's children and your flocks and your herds and all you have. There I will provide for you." And in Genesis 50:20, Joseph repeats the promise : "As for you, you meant evil against me, but God meant it for good to bring about that many people should be kept alive. So do not fear, I will provide for you and your little ones." Joseph chooses not to destroy his brothers, because he has come to understand that God has a plan, God's plan involves their sin, and God, in his love, is using their sin to rescue them. Who is Joseph to stand in the way of the mercy and redemption of God?

The Substance of Joseph's Forgiveness

There is a danger in paying lip service to forgiveness. Joseph is not doing that. When we are wronged, there is a big difference between saying, "It is fine. Whatever," and saying, "I forgive you." Some of us are in relationships right now and know those relationships are broken but the other people do not know because we have said, "It is fine. Whatever," but we really have not forgiven. Joseph is not doing that. Joseph means what he says. Joseph is not just saying, "Thirteen years. Whatever. Live and let live," while thinking to himself, *I hate them.* He asks his brothers to move to where he is. He tells them he will protect them. He will take care of them. He comforts them, kisses them, cries over them, hugs them. There is real substance to this forgiveness. It is not a passive-aggressive trap. It is not "Whatever. Fine. Let's just move on with life." It is true forgiveness. And lest we think Joseph has to forgive his brothers for the sake of his father, Joseph gets a second opportunity to punish his brothers after his father's death. He doesn't take the bait.

Joseph's forgiveness and subsequent care are like saying to the abusive family member, "Please, move in with me." Joseph's actions are like saying to the former business partner who screwed you over, "Sorry to hear you got laid off. Come work with me." Joseph's words are like saying to the former friend who betrayed you, "Come spend the holidays at my house. Let me cook for you. Let me feed you. Let me celebrate with you." This forgiveness is not lip service. It is not fake or phony. It is real, substantive forgiveness, and it comes from Joseph's understanding of God's plan.

The Substitution for Joseph's Forgiveness

This passage is very powerful, but it is also very dangerous. We can only understand this passage when we understand who we are in the story. With which character should we relate? Most preachers, most religions, and most people in general would say we are the Joseph in this story and if we aren't Joseph, we should strive to be him. We hear things like "We need to forgive like Joseph. We should get our forgiveness from an understanding of a bigger picture. We need to forgive in a real and substantive way." But let me sound a warning: If we read this story and think we are Joseph, we will absolutely destroy our lives.

How will we destroy our lives? First, if we think we are Joseph, we will come to believe that every instance of evil in our life is a part of God's revealed plan of redemption as it relates to his people. We will come to think that the time we were sexually assaulted; the time gossip destroyed our reputations; when we were cheated, robbed, hurt, or damaged was the revealed plan of God. Nowhere in the book of Genesis are we told that every instance of evil is somehow connected to God's larger plan. What we do see in Joseph's story, and throughout the book of Genesis, is that the sins of people cannot undermine or thwart God's plan of redemption for his people.

In Genesis 2, we see God's plan. His plan is a perfect world where Adam and Eve cultivate, create, and fill the earth. Sin and evil come into the world when Adam and Eve eat from the tree, and that evil spawns and regenerates at a rapid pace. Adam and Eve's rebellion is contrary to God's revealed plan in Scripture. When God shows up to Cain, he does not congratulate Cain for killing Abel and suggest that they forget about it and move forward (Genesis 4:1–16). When Lamech boasts of killing a little boy and sings a song about it, when he takes two wives and begins to subjugate women, that is not part of God's plan (Genesis 4:18–24). Instead, the author is showing us the rapid decay of the world through these stories. When God floods the world, it is in judgment for evil. God does not say, "Oh, the world has descended into chaos and evil, exactly where I want it." He floods the earth because of his disgust for evil.

In the midst of this evil, Joseph is connected to the promise of God through Abraham, Isaac, and Jacob. He has a 30,000-foot view of his life because he knows the promises made to his great-grandfather, grandfather, and father. He is able to rest in the promise God made to preserve his family and to use his family to restore the world. God had to get Joseph to Egypt to do that. Joseph can clearly see that his brothers' evil was used to get him to Egypt to continue with this plan. The plan of God is not about figuring out the purpose for every instance of evil in our lives. It is about overcoming evil. Great harm has been done to many people by well-meaning Christians who run around telling people that evil is all part of the revealed plan of God. The evil done to us is contrary to God's character, however. He despises it more than we do. In the midst of evil, our primary response is not to seek to know and explain its meaning as it relates to a larger plan but to place our hope in the plan of God that there will one day be a world where no one suffers any evil any longer (Revelation 21:1–4).

If we substitute ourselves for Joseph, we will also believe that the only time we can forgive anyone is when we are able to see how their act corresponds to the plan of God, that when we can sit down and map out how their acts brought us to a "better" place in God's plan, then we can forgive. One problem with that thinking: We are almost never going to be able to do that in our lives. People who have never suffered and never been victims are the people who naively believe we can build maps to understand these acts and their painful results. In their minds, we can mathematically make sense of it all. But those of us who have actually been hurt know it is not enough to simply say, "I see how in six moves, I will be a stronger person." If we are waiting on divine understanding or a divine map in order to forgive, then we will never be able to reconcile any relationship. If someone comes to us and says, "I am sorry," we are going to say, "OK. But before I forgive, I need to write a five-page paper about how you wronged me and why it had to happen in order to make me the person I am today, so I can use the pain to help others with their pain. Then maybe I will forgive you." That is never going to happen. They are not going to have those answers for us, and we are not going to have those answers for ourselves. Many religions, many religious people, and even many Christians have tried to use this logic. But God's plan is not that we must suffer evil in order to teach others after us how to suffer evil effectively.

Most importantly, we cannot read ourselves into Joseph because we are not that innocent. We want to read ourselves into Joseph because it is so tempting to embrace a worldview in which everyone has sinned against us, where they must come to us and ask us for forgiveness. With this worldview, we do not have to go to anyone to ask forgiveness because we are not the cause of the broken relationships in our lives; the broken world is something that happens to us and is never caused by us. With this worldview, we sit with power as kings as our perpetrators come begging for mercy.

Yes, there are some situations in life when we are actually only victims, but to reduce ourselves down to only victims all the time is to be completely and utterly dishonest with ourselves and with the world. If we read ourselves into Joseph, it will destroy us. Reading ourselves into Joseph will destroy our faith, if it has not already.

If we are not Joseph in this story, who are we? We are the brothers. We are the brothers who have, at every turn, betrayed God by living out a story other than God's story. By ignoring God's commands and law, by ignoring the grace he shows us every moment, we betray him. More specifically, we see ourselves as Joseph's brothers in the story of Jesus Christ. In Christ, God came down to Earth as a man, as a king-like Joseph, only greater, and we rejected him and crucified him. No, we did not commit that exact crime; we were not physically present at the scene where it happened in history, but there is no difference between us denying God authority over our sex lives and people presiding over Christ's crucifixion. Both are attempts to silence and kill God so we can live outside of his authority.

When we think about the resurrected Jesus Christ, the King, we should be terrified when we hear Jesus say, "All authority has been given to me" (Matthew 28:18). It is as terrifying as being one of Joseph's brothers and hearing him say, "It is me, Joseph! Remember me? I run Egypt now!" If Jesus has all authority, and if we rejected this King's authority, we should be terrified, yet through the power of the Gospel, Jesus says, "I do not hate you. I love you. God has a plan. God is using your evil to bring about your rescue." When Jesus came to the earth, he went to the cross for our evil; he was crucified for our evil. And when he rose from the dead, God verified that he used our own sin to rescue us from the power of this sin. Jesus stood, just as Joseph once stood, and said, "Do you not see, even though you willfully were doing evil, how God used this evil to provide rescue for you on the cross?" The good news of the Gospel is that, much like Joseph's brothers, we can be forgiven. The Gospel is not a call to go out and forgive like Joseph and if we fail, then we will be abandoned. Because of the Gospel, we have a King who ought to have destroyed us but died for us instead. This King has come back from the dead to provide for us and take care of us.

To be a Christian is to see Jesus in Joseph's power and in his loving disposition toward his brothers. We ought to be terrified of a King whom we have wronged and terrified for the times we have come to him and said that our religion or our moral goodness should get us off the hook. God sees right through all those arguments and says to us, "No, it is because of the better Joseph, the true King, Jesus, who died and rose from the dead and serves you, that you are spared." The hope of reconciling the world is not that we would go out and try to emulate Joseph's forgiveness, as though we could, as though we have a reservoir of forgiveness from which we can continually draw. The good news of the Gospel is that the language of reconciliation is grace and that we become fluent in that language by meeting, worshiping, and spending time with the person of Jesus.

The only hope for reconciliation in the world is to understand that God is reconciling us to him through Jesus. Only then can we go out into the world, into our broken relationships, families, and careers, and offer grace, even if we have the opportunity to crush people. When we run dry of that forgiveness, we run right back to Jesus, who promises he will provide for us. He will love us and fill us back up so we can return to the world with love because we have been reconciled to God. We can be gracious because we have been shown grace. We can show love instead of judgment because we have received love instead of judgment. We cannot forgive like Joseph. Even Joseph could not forgive like Joseph. That is why he needed a snapshot into God's cosmic plan. Only then could he forgive as he did. We have received that kind of forgiveness, and we also have that kind of snapshot in the person of Jesus.

Whether we think we are victimizer or victim, the truth is, we are both, though not in every situation. Some of us are real victims in many situations, and all of us are victimizers to one degree or another. If we define ourselves by the people we hurt, our only hope is that we can learn the language of reconciliation at the feet of the King who, though he ought to crush us, instead was crushed for us. That is our only hope. We deserve judgment, but we are offered grace. If we define ourselves by the wrongs done to us, before we can ever forgive the one who wronged us, we must first do business with the one we have wronged. Grace is primarily an inward experience before it is an outward extension. If we do not experience the grace of the one we have victimized, namely Christ, then we are never going to be able to extend grace. But it is possible to extend real grace, real forgiveness, real reconciliation, as we are changed by the grace and reconciliation that we have received from God through Christ. We can become conduits to others, but not until we first sit at the feet of God and learn the language of the one who displayed the ultimate grace in his life, death, and resurrection. We want to be Joseph, and many people will tell us that we are, but we are not. There is a greater Joseph, and his name is Jesus.

CPSIA information can be obtained at www.ICGtesting.com
Printed in the USA
BVOW06s1332130416

444062BV00026B/359/P